# CONTROLLING
# NUCLEAR WEAPONS

THE FRANK W. ABRAMS LECTURES

Stanley Hoffmann. *Duties Beyond Borders: On the Limits and Possibilities of Ethical International Politics.* 1981.
James S. Coleman. *The Asymmetric Society.* 1982.
Guido Calabresi. *Ideals, Beliefs, Attitudes, and the Law.* 1985.
Robert Dahl. *Controlling Nuclear Weapons: Democracy Versus Guardianship.* 1985.

# CONTROLLING NUCLEAR WEAPONS

## Democracy Versus Guardianship

### ROBERT DAHL

SYRACUSE UNIVERSITY PRESS
1985

First Edition

**Library of Congress Cataloging in Publication Data**

Dahl, Robert Alan, 1915–
  Controlling nuclear weapons ; democracy versus
guardianship.

  (Frank W. Abrams lectures)
  Bibliography: p.
  Includes index.
  1. Authoritarianism.   2. Democracy.   3. Nuclear
arms control.   I. Title.   II. Series.
JC481.D33   1985        321.9        85-4783
ISBN 0-8156-2334-8
ISBN 0-8156-0196-4 (pbk.)

*Manufactured in the United States of America*

# Contents

ROBERT DAHL is Sterling Professor of Political Science at Yale University and the author of *Pluralist Democracy in the United States* and *Dilemmas of Pluralist Democracy, Autonomy Versus Control.*

# Foreword

THE ABRAMS LECTURE SERIES has added a new and substantial component to the richness of academic life at Syracuse University. The 1984 series by Robert Dahl sparked great interest among members of the faculty and the student body.

The Abrams Lecture Series is financed by a grant from the Exxon Education Foundation in memory of the late Frank W. Abrams, former chairman of the board of the Standard Oil Company (New Jersey), the predecessor of Exxon, and former chairman of the board of trustees of Syracuse University.

A member of Syracuse University's Class of 1912, Mr. Abrams was a life-long leader in support of higher education. He was a founder of the Council for Financial Aid to Education, chairman of the Ford Foundation's Fund for the Advancement of Education, and a trustee for the Alfred E. Sloan Foundation.

Mr. Abrams was one of the key pioneers who awakened American business, both through education and landmark legal precedents, to the need for financial support by business for private higher education. It was a contribution by Mr. Abrams, the importance of which cannot be overemphasized, which makes it particularly appropriate that this lecture series be presented in his name.

A special thank you is due the members of the Abrams Lecture Series Planning Committee, headed by Guthrie S. Birkhead, Dean of the Maxwell Graduate School of Citizenship and Public

Affairs. Working with Dean Birkhead are Michael O. Sawyer, Vice Chancellor of the University and Professor of Constitutional Law; L. Richard Oliker, Dean of the School of Management; Richard D. Schwartz, Ernest I. White Professor of Law; Chris J. Witting, Chairman of the Syracuse University Board of Trustees; and Robert L. Payton, President of the Exxon Education Foundation.

MELVIN A. EGGERS
Chancellor
Syracuse University

# Acknowledgments

I WISH TO EXPRESS my profound appreciation to Syracuse University for their invitation to deliver the Abrams Lectures, which gave me the opportunity to present the argument of this book. I also want to thank Marc Lendler, David Priebe, and Dawn Rossit for their research assistance on several of the topics touched on in the book.

# CONTROLLING
# NUCLEAR WEAPONS

# Introduction

IT IS TESTIMONY to the power of the democratic idea in the present world that, with few exceptions, even in the most flagrantly undemocratic countries leaders generally portray their regimes as transitional systems that will someday eventuate in democracy — usually some "higher order" of cleansed or purified democracy. That they should feel compelled to do so, presumably in order to enhance their own legitimacy, is historically quite recent. Until this century, leaders in undemocratic regimes would ordinarily have felt no need to acknowledge the ultimate superiority of the democratic ideal in order to clothe their own rule in a mantle of legitimacy.

This nearly universal appeal of democracy as an ultimate ideal today should be heartening to advocates of democracy. Yet two important qualifications immediately leap to mind: First, most regimes in the present world are not democratic. Even by the rather generous standards we must use when applying the term to the United States, the countries of western Europe, Japan, and others, only about forty countries out of approximately 150 can reasonably be said to have democratic political systems. Second, leaders in many, perhaps most, nondemocratic regimes justify their claim to rule at least transitionally by appealing, in some form, to an argument of great antiquity and ubiquity. The argument is that at least in the particular time and place, but per-

1

haps more generally, the average person is not sufficiently competent to govern, while, on the other hand, a minority of persons, consisting of the best qualified, *are* distinctly more competent to rule, and so ought to rule over the rest. This is, in essence, Plato's argument in *The Republic* for a system of guardianship. Leaders who proclaim this view usually contend that they, naturally, are among the minority of exceptionally able people who ought to exercise guardianship over the rest.

For those of us who believe in democracy, it is tempting to dismiss an argument like this as utterly unwarranted. It is perhaps even more tempting to assume that the "Good Housekeeping seal of approval" given in this century to the superiority of democracy — as an ideal, if not necessarily as a goal for here and now — has pretty much settled the question.

But to draw this conclusion would, I think, be a grave mistake. Instead, we — that is to say, advocates of democracy — need to confront this ancient and ubiquitous argument anew and directly. Paradoxically, we ought to do so not because it persists as a rationalization for contemporary authoritarian governments, but rather because in democratic countries the complexity of public issues challenges the assumption that ordinary people are competent to make decisions about these matters.

Consider a few contemporary issues in this country: What are we to do about nuclear waste disposal? Should recombinant DNA research be regulated by the government? If so, how? The problem of nuclear reactor safety and the trade offs between the risks and gains of nuclear power are much more complex than the simple solutions offered on all sides would suggest. Or consider the technical and economic issues involved in clean air. At what point do the costs of auto emissions control exceed the gains? How and to what point should industrial pollution be regulated? For example, should electric utilities be required to convert to clean burning fuels, or to install stack scrubbers? How serious a problem is ozone depletion, and what should be done about it?

If these issues are obviously technical and difficult, consider the complexity of some more familiar matters. How should we deal with the huge federal deficit? Indeed, should we deal with it or simply ignore it instead? What are we to do about the problem of health care, hospital costs, the financing of Medicare and

Medicaid? Or the military budget? We could quickly think of many other such questions.

What problems like these have in common is that they have enormously important consequences for a vast number of people, they seem to require government decisions of some kind, and in order to make wise decisions, decision makers need specialized knowledge that most citizens do not possess.

One might respond by saying that even in a democracy, after all, complex decisions like these can be delegated to experts. But suppose that most of us do not even possess enough knowledge to understand the terms on which we can safely delegate authority over these decisions to those more expert than we? Then we have not simply *delegated* authority. Instead, we have *alienated* control over our lives to others: that is, for practical purposes we simply lose control over crucial decisions, and lose control over our lives. The more we alienate authority, rather than delegate it on terms that allow us to retain a meaningful degree of final control, the more we lose our freedom, and the more hollow the democratic process becomes. Or to put it in another way, the more that we alienate authority the more the external forms of democracy clothe a *de facto* regime of guardianship.

Perhaps no public question poses the challenge of guardianship more starkly than American policies concerning nuclear weapons. Nuclear weapons present a tragic paradox: No decisions can be more fateful for Americans, and for the world, than decisions about nuclear weapons. Yet these decisions have largely escaped the control of the democratic process.

Admittedly, the control of nuclear weapons is an extreme case, not a representative one. Nonetheless, it serves to illustrate a general problem of extraordinary importance to all of us who believe in the possibility of democracy: Are the institutions of contemporary democracy adequate to cope satisfactorily with the enormous complexity of public matters?

|

# Obstacles to Democratic Control

## CONFLICTING PRINCIPLES: DEMOCRACY OR GUARDIANSHIP?

THE DEMOCRATIC PROCESS is generally believed to be justified on the ground that people are entitled to participate as political equals in making binding decisions, enforced by the state, on matters that have important consequences for their individual and collective interests. Nothing can have more important consequences for so many people, Americans and others alike, as decisions that may prevent or cause the use of nuclear weapons. If it is also true that these decisions have so far been arrived at pretty much outside the reach of democratic controls, then we must count this a profound failure in the capacity of contemporary democratic institutions to achieve their purposes. Though I speak here specifically of the United States, the failure is common to other democratic countries as well.

I do not say that policies would necessarily have been substantially different if a more democratic process had operated, nor, certainly, that they have been made in opposition to a public consensus favoring other policies. They have simply been arrived at without even the ordinary constraints of the democratic process.

Yet the failure on nuclear weapons is not unique. Rather it is indicative of a general weakness of the democratic process —

5

failure may be too severe a term — in dealing with highly complex questions, no matter how momentous they may be. Control over nuclear decisions is emblematic of a larger issue, and American experience will serve to illustrate a problem that no democratic country, to my knowledge, has solved.

Have we then reached an inherent limit on democracy, a fundamental and inescapable defect? If so, are we rationally obliged, no matter how much our deepest feelings may tug us away from the dismaying conclusion, to commit ourselves to a nondemocratic alternative, at least over some set of public policies of which policies about nuclear weapons are perhaps only an extreme example? Or is the defect rather to be located in our political institutions, or more generally in the political institutions distinctive to modern democracy?

The first question invites us to choose between two conflicting assumptions. One is that, taken all around, adults are adequately qualified to participate in making the collective decisions that they will be required to obey, as with laws, and that no minority among them is so clearly better qualified that its members are entitled to make all collective decisions. This assumption does not exclude the possibility that people may choose to delegate some collective decisions to others whom they think to be better qualified in the particular instance. It does imply that the citizens are qualified to judge which questions require delegation, to set the terms on which the delegation is to take place, and to recapture the delegated authority when they choose. In short, the assumption allows for delegation of authority but not its alienation. Let me call this assumption the Strong Principle of Equality.

The alternative assumption is that generally speaking most adults are not qualified to make binding collective decisions, whereas a minority among them is well qualified to do so, or at least in some conditions could be. Drawing on Plato's term for his rulers in *The Republic*, we might call this assumption the Principle of Guardianship, or if one prefers a word of recent coinage, the Principle of Meritocratic Rulership.

One might object that in practice democratic countries employ a principle of meritocracy in their bureaucracies, and that the political system of a modern democratic country is a combination of democracy and meritocracy. This is of course true. It is a fact of life that I shall come back to frequently. But we must not allow this important fact of life to obscure the fundamental conflict between the two principles. The Strong Principle of Equality, remember, permits delegation of authority. It is therefore not inconsistent with that principle to delegate authority to a bureaucracy that is itself organized on meritocratic principles. But it would be inconsistent if *de jure* delegation were to become *de facto* alienation. And that is precisely the problem: We have in fact turned over to a small group of people decisions of incalculable importance to ourselves and mankind, and it is very far from clear how, if at all, we could recapture a control that in fact we have never had. Thus in this crucial area, and there may be others, we have perhaps unwittingly adopted the Principle of Guardianship.

I realize that given the political culture of this country the Guardians may resist being identified as such. James Schlesinger, who would qualify as one of the guardians, reacted with some asperity to certain remarks of William Colby, a former director of the Central Intelligence Agency, suggesting the existence of a "nuclear priesthood." "I get restless, and I suspect others do too, over firebrand comments about a supposed nuclear priesthood. Bill knows better than that. Discussions regarding nuclear strategy have been quite open, more so than in intelligence matters and Bill would properly resent casual remarks about an intelligence priesthood," as reported in *The New York Times*, June 14, 1983, p. 20.

Discussions regarding nuclear strategy have until recently taken place among only a very tiny proportion of the American population. Among that minute group the number who have had a significant impact on actual decisions is very much smaller. The proportions may be somewhat larger than in the Soviet Union but that is only to say that in the one country the guardians are, to use Mr. Schlesinger's word, somewhat more open than in the other.

That decisions on nuclear strategy and on other complex issues are made by the few rather than the many—quite likely even by a meritorious few—is not simply a consequence of an effort to prevent discussion and participation by a broader and more representative selection of the *demos*, though that may be part of the explanation. If only that were true, however, solutions would be much easier to suggest. But it is instead mainly a consequence of the fact that the democratic process is not well equipped to deal with questions of exceptional complexity. That is why the problem will defy simple solutions.


## THE SIMPLE THEORY OF DEMOCRATIC REPRESENTATION

A reasoned justification for the democratic process rests on the assumption that ordinary people are adequately qualified to govern themselves. This assumption remains at the heart of democratic beliefs, even though democratic institutions have changed enormously over the centuries. In particular, the institutions for dealing with complex issues have changed radically and have themselves become highly complex.

When democracy was first consciously identified as a distinctive kind of regime among Greeks in the fifty century before the present era, the most important locus of policy making was the citizen assembly, the town meeting of classical democracy. Although it would be an exaggeration to say that all decisions were made in the assembly—in Athens the agenda was prepared by a subcommittee of the Boule, the Council of Five Hundred—it was there that all the important policies bearing on the life of the city were debated and decided. Although every citizen could attend and in principle anyone who attended could speak, many did not attend and in a city as large as Athens most of those who attended would have participated only in the voting and in manifesting approval or disdain for the remarks of a speaker. For expert knowledge and wise decisions, citizens depended on their own common sense and on those of their fellow citizens in whom they recognized special experience or wisdom. Although like every other political system that has ever existed Greek democracies made mistakes — the fateful expedition to Sicily defended in the assembly by no less a man than Pericles was a colossal disaster — on the whole they appear to have acted about as wisely as can be expected: which is to say that there do not appear to have been huge gaps between the judgments made by the assembly and the views of leaders, like Pericles, whom we with the benefit of hindsight can say were among the wisest and most public spirited.

Because the notion of assembly democracy dominated democratic ideas for two thousand years, it is not surprising that it persists, buried beneath the detritus of historic memory, as an easily awakened vision of ideal democracy. Consequently when, in the eighteenth century and later, representation was joined to the theory and practice of democracy, some advocates of democracy regarded representatives at best as mere agents of the will of their fellow citizens and, at worst, as did Rousseau in *The Social Contract*, as totally illegitimate. Others, however, took the view, which became increasingly acceptable, that representatives could refine the popular will by adding greater knowledge to the often rawly formed will of the people. Frequently the process of refinement, even of transformation, was particularly assigned to an upper chamber whose members were more insulated from the citizens.

Yet another layer of presumed expertness came to be grafted on to democratic theory and practice in the late nineteenth century, one that was to gather incredible momentum in the century that followed: bureaucracies. In the orthodox theory, these were presented as neutral experts with authority delegated by the legislature (and in the United States by the chief executive) to transmute into the most efficient means the objectives expressed by the will of the people, as refined by their elected representatives.

Meanwhile another institutional development had been taking place that was to reach its fullest expression in the American congress. This was the system of committees in which members of the legislature could themselves acquire a degree of expertise often rivalling and even surpassing that of the administrative officials. Since about the middle of this century, the committees in Congress have in turn taken to hiring their own expert staffs, thus adding still another circuit to the already complex circuitry that loads specialized information and knowledge on to the signals generated by public opinion.

A simplified description of the way in which a modern democratic system ideally handles complex questions might then look something like this: By means of elections, to which citizens bring judgments about past performance and likely future performance of candidates, the citizen body or a majority thereof determines the fundamental goals that elected officials will pursue. Determining the best means to achieve these goals is a process of successive approximation during which the set of possible means is progressively reduced by considerations of feasibility and efficiency based on expert knowledge, beginning with the committees in Congress and ending with the choice of specific means by experts in the relevant agency. From the electorate to the most specialized expert, the whole process relies heavily on making changes incrementally, which provides opportunities for feedback and the accumulation of information, knowledge, experience, and learning. Although not common, occasionally a certain amount of deliberate experimentation is possible. In this way even highly complex issues may be disposed of by a process that, although radically different from the original vision of democracy and its simple institutions, is nonetheless a satisfactory adaptation of that vision to a world of infinite complexity which the Greeks twenty five centuries ago in a much simpler age — or for that matter, our predecessors in the eighteenth century — could never have imagined.

## DIFFICULTIES

Regrettably the simple theory just summarized is — like most simple theories about politics — unsatisfactory. To begin with, the issues that arise in campaigns and elections nowadays are always numerous and often complex, indeed sometimes, as with nuclear weapons, inordinately complicated. Thus voters are not confronted with a clear, neat pair of easily grasped alternatives, even though in cognitive desperation they may force the horrid complexity of the issues into a more understandable clean-cut choice. However, as a consequence of the number and complexity of the issues, it is frequently impossible to determine objectively what policies a majority of voters may have intended to support or oppose. Politicians impose their own meaning on the election outcome, and the victors naturally interpret the results as a vindication of their views. American presidents invariably discover in the tea leaves a "mandate" for their policies. Although the mandate is largely mythical it is an extraordinarily powerful myth.

Moreover, in a world where changes occur as rapidly as in ours, new issues, sometimes vaguely foreseen, sometimes totally unexpected, arise between elections. As a result, the boundaries around policy choices set by elections become even more indeterminate.

The ambiguity and indeterminacy of elections are further increased by uncertainties in the relation of means to ends. How fortunate it would be for the democratic process if the electorate could clearly specify its ends or goals and trust experts and technicians to choose the most efficient instruments for attaining these goals. But the relation bewteen ends and means, or goals and techniques, is nothing like as straightforward as the simple theory assumes. It has often been noted that means are not always sharply distinguishable from ends, that what we take as an end may itself be a means to a further and perhaps more obscure end, and that means may not be coolly neutral but packed with end values. Campaigns and elections never present a crisply outlined choice between conflicting values — freedom versus equality, love of country versus love of humanity, and so on. More often than not, candidates are indistinguishable, at least in rhetoric, in their attachments to such fundamental values. Office-seeking politicians do not explicitly differ so much over ultimate ends as on the means they claim will best achieve these ends. I do not think that I have ever heard a candidate, or anyone else for that matter, say that he preferred war to peace, real peace, anyway. Political issues are predominantly about means, and voters are compelled to choose between differing proposals as to the best means to achieve their ultimate ends. Arguments about means can get fearfully hard to follow.

For these reasons if for no others, experts cannot be trusted to choose the means to broadly specified goals, for in choosing the means they would in effect determine the ends. What is more, even acknowledged experts rarely agree in their assessments of the risks entailed in a policy, the relative likelihood of different outcomes, and the costs and benefits of alternative policies. To all this confusion, ambiguity, and complexity must be added the effects of bureaucratic dynamics. Officials in government agencies are

not themselves perfectly neutral technicians dispassionately searching for the policy that would maximize the values affirmed by
the electorate. Officials are also politicians with ambitions for
themselves and their agencies. Nowhere is the play of bureaucratic
dynamics more evident than in service rivalries over budgets,
weapons, and strategic plans.

Finally, on some matters incremental adaptations of a policy, as experience is gained with its results, works badly and experiment is impossible. American entry into the mire of Vietnam
was incremental, but feedback was badly distorted or misinter-
preted.


## THE EXTENDED ADVERSARIAL PROCESS

In some circumstances the difficulties just noted can be reduced
by the operation of an adversarial process that typically, but by
no means inevitably, occurs in democratic political systems. Sometimes, though not always, that process takes place within limits
set by a fairly widespread agreement among citizens on the relevant goals a policy should try to reach: for example, improving
or maintaining the quality of the natural environment even at a
modest cost to business, consumers, and taxpayers.

Suppose that alternative policies are reduced essentially to
two, and that, as is often the case, the two alternatives are the
policy of the administration and the policy of the opposition. Suppose further that a pretty substantial number of citizens are at
least moderately well informed about the issue and have fairly
definite views as to which of the two policies they prefer. In addition, suppose that a plentiful number of acknowledged experts
and scientists express views that are readily accessible to citizens,
perhaps through the aid of interest group leaders who, though not
quite as knowledgeable as the scientists, are nevertheless exceptionally well informed about the issue. Imagine also that, as often
happens, both inside and outside the government the people most
closely involved in decisions about the policy in question are more
or less divided into two opposing groups, such as those favoring
the administration's policy and critics of the administration who

support an opposing policy. Finally, we can readily imagine that it might be to the advantage of members of Congress to take up the cudgels on this issue, particularly if they are members of the relevant House or Senate committee.

Under these conditions the adversarial process, broadly extended to include a hefty segment of the general public, might actually produce a fair approximation to the process described in the simple theory: The issue poses a choice between two alternatives. The policy elites, polarized into two groups, find it advantageous to seek support in the wider public. Controversy, discussion, debate, hearings in congressional committees help both to inform the public and to mobilize citizens and interest group leaders to make their views known and to bring pressures to bear on policymakers. Because a good number of citizens are moderately well informed and in touch with well-informed leaders and subleaders, and because the experts and policy elites are openly contesting the policies espoused by their adversaries, their judgments are not so plastic that they are easily manipulated by the policy elites. If the issue remains alive and salient through a time of campaigning and elections, majority views may be translated into the policies of the congress and the president.

It is difficult to say how often something like this does take place, but I suspect that for the reasons already mentioned more often than not it fails to occur. In any case, American policies concerning nuclear weapons were made for the better part of thirty five years with hardly a trace of an adversarial process except occasionally among a minuscule policy elite.


## NUCLEAR WEAPONS AND AMERICAN POLITICS

Decisions about nuclear weapons and strategy elude democratic controls because the essential conditions for both the simple theory of democratic representation and the adversarial process are largely absent. To begin with, the issues are immensely complex. The complexities are roughly of three kinds: technical, political, and moral. Although I am going to postpone discussion of the moral complexities until Chapter 3, let me say a word about the others.

Numerous crucial technical questions about nuclear weapons and strategy are all far outside the realm of ordinary experience. They require specialized knowledge, some of it both intricate and secret, that ordinary citizens not only do not possess but cannot reasonably be expected to possess. They include such questions as the effects of various weapons, their reliability and accuracy, whether and how they can be detected or their existence verified, the relative balance of forces between the United States and its allies on the one hand and the Union of Soviet Socialist Republics and its allies on the other.

Equally if not more difficult are the political questions. What *is* Soviet policy? What are the intentions of Soviet leaders? What risks will they take, and in what circumstances? The same questions asked of U.S. leaders are not much easier to answer. For example, there are reasons for thinking that some civilian officials and military officers in the Department of Defense believe that nuclear war is a realistic option. How much influence do these people have on strategic planning? Few of us can know the answer; members of the attentive public can, at best, only guess at the answer.

An overwhelming proportion of the American people, however, agree that a fundamental objective should be to avoid nuclear war, as, I believe, do most people with any significant influence on policy. If the conditions required by the simple theory of democratic representation existed, then policy makers equipped with expert knowledge would proceed, through a process of successively narrowing down the alternative means to this end, to adopt the technically best solution. But alas for the simple theory and for democratic values, means and ends are inextricably tangled. In order to make judgments about means the experts must necessarily make judgments about values. To make matters worse, the experts do not agree either on key technical questions or, it appears, on the relative weight they assign to different values.

To illustrate the point, let me touch briefly on a discussion more fully explored in Chapter 3. Most people in this country would probably prefer a strategy of deterrence to either a preemptive first strike at Soviet launching sites or unilateral disarmament. This choice in itself is one of daunting complexity. But putting the other alternatives completely to one side for the moment, even if we assume that a policy of deterrence is most likely to prevent nuclear war, we must still confront several alternatives that completely intermix technical and moral issues. For example, should we target only the Soviet launching sites, in order to avoid the indiscriminate killing of civilians? Or should we also target the headquarters of the military and civilian leadership, in the hope of terminating a war more swiftly by destroying the Soviet command structure — even though this policy would require us to target some cities? Or to maximize deterrence, since our supply of weapons far exceeds what could be used against launching sites, should we straightforwardly target a substantial part of the city population of the Soviet Union, horrendous as the results would be if the strategy of deterrence should ever fail?

Finally, in the case of nuclear weapons strategy we cannot count on learning about the alternatives by means of experiments or incremental policy decisions. The only genuine experiment would be the disaster that everyone wants to avoid, while incremental fine tuning of the dosage of destruction is a fantasy for war gaming but not for the real world. When we know with reasonable certainty what the consequences of our nuclear strategy are, it will be too late to change it, and a great many of us will not be around to appreciate the wisdom gained at infinite cost from that catastrophic experience.

If the conditions for the simple theory of democratic representation to hold have been absent, they have also not been favorable for the operation of the extended adversarial process. For one thing, an overwhelming proportion of the citizen body has until quite recently totally abdicated its rights to participate in any way in making nuclear decisions even of the most general sort. The complexities described here, the deep though mainly unacknowledged fears activated by the danger of nuclear war, and a trust in the officials in charge to do what is right, have until recently pushed the crucial questions involved in nuclear decisions well outside the conscious attention and concern of most citizens. (See Appendix 1 for some evidence on this point.)

Consequently, decisions have been entrusted exclusively to officials in the executive branch, sometimes with the participation of a few members of Congress. Of course the adversarial process has sometimes occurred within the policy elites. But there it takes place veiled from public view. To a participant like James Schlesinger, those disputes may well seem relatively "open," at least compared to differences within the intelligence community. But surely not even he would contend that immeasurably consequential decisions, even following internal controversy, taken by an infinitesimally small percentage of citizens, satisfy the requirements of the democratic process. The question under examination at the moment, remember, is not whether the decisions have been wise. The issue is whether they have been made by anything like even a rough approximation to the democratic process. It seems obvious that they have not.

Earlier I suggested that decisions about nuclear weapons policies represent an extreme instance of a more general problem, the existence of political issues that are at once so crucial and yet so complex that they tend to elude the kinds of democratic controls that the institutions of modern democratic countries were designed to achieve. The result is that small groups of decision makers exercise a degree of influence over decisions that, from a democratic perspective, is excessive and illicit. This does not mean that a single cohesive elite makes all these decisions. Quite the contrary: as Schlesinger contends, even within a particular sphere like nuclear weapons, the people who exercise significant influence on policies, whether officials, advisers, or critics, often express sharply conflicting views. Moreover, the influential policy makers in one sphere frequently arrive at their decisions independently of policy makers in other spheres. Indeed, the lack of coordination among policy makers resulting from the relative autonomy of decision making in the different spheres is considered by many observers to be a serious defect.

However that may be, the democratic process has clearly failed to function in controlling what may well be the most important decisions that will ever be made on this earth. Because of the boundless complexity of the issues involved in these decisions, perhaps the democratic process is inherently incapable of controlling them, and others of similar complexity. At least we must look that possibility square in the face and consider whether there may not be a better alternative.

## CONCLUSION

If we were to conclude that the democratic process is bound to fail us here, what should take its place? One option would be to acknowledge openly that a small policy elite *should* continue to make all the important decisions on nuclear weapons and strategy. In this way, we could convert a fact of life into a norm. What is, at present, a violation of democratic standards, and thus presumably of American political philosophy and values, might then perhaps be perceived and accepted as meeting a different standard of political excellence: that it is better for decisions to be wise than to be democratic. But since decisions about nuclear weapons represent only an extreme instance of a general phenomenon that modern democracies seem to be unable to cope with democratically — the existence of political issues that are both crucially important and inordinately complex — this principle, it would seem, should be extended to a broad range of significant issues.

One can readily imagine a hybrid political system in which democratic controls function more or less effectively in some spheres of policy, while other spheres are governed by meritocratic elites, or guardians, free from democratic controls. To the extent that highly complex issues now elude democratic controls, that hybrid already exists, at least in a rude way. The justification for such a hybrid would be that in some spheres of great importance and complexity, policies are not likely to be both wise and democratic, and it is better that they be wise though undemocratic than democratic but unwise.

In some policy areas, arguably the criterion of wisdom *should* take precedence over the criterion of democracy. The argument that rulers should above all possess the capacity for making wise and virtuous decisions, and that they cannot make wise and virtuous decisions if they are subject to democratic controls, is ancient. It is the argument of guardianship. The philosophic ideal of guardianship has been offered as an alternative to democracy for nearly as long as the democratic ideal itself has existed and doubtless in unphilosophic form gave legitimacy to regimes long before democracy appeared.

The next chapter will explore the general argument for a state governed by guardians to see whether it provides a better alternative than the democratic process. As we shall discover, the case for guardianship looks rather persuasive, at least for matters of great technical and moral complexity. But before concluding that for us to act responsibly in a fearfully complicated world is so difficult that we should turn over the responsibility to more qualified guardians, we had better take a hard look at the risks of guardianship, as we shall in Chapter 3.

And if those risks look to be excessive, then we should ask ourselves whether there may not be ways of redesigning democratic institutions so that the ancient vision of a people governing itself might remain relevant even in this complicated world, where it is our destiny to live together — or, failing that, to die together.

# 2

# The Case for Guardianship

A PERENNIAL ALTERNATIVE to democracy is government by meritocratic rulers[1] or guardians. Most beautifully and enduringly presented by Plato in *The Republic*[2] the idea of guardianship has exerted a powerful pull throughout human history. Although it is often used in its most vulgar form as a rationalization for corrupt, brutal, and inept authoritarian regimes of all kinds, the argument for it does not fall simply because it has been badly abused. If we were to apply the same harsh test to democratic ideas they too would be found wanting. We should confront the case for guardianship without employing guilt by association to undermine its appeal at the outset.

## VISIONS OF GUARDIANSHIP

The idea of guardianship has appealed to a great variety of political thinkers and leaders in many different guises and in many different parts of the world over most of recorded history. If Plato provides perhaps the most familiar example, the practical ideal of Confucius, who was born more than a century before Plato, has had far more profound influence over many more people and persists to the present day, deeply embedded in the cultures of several countries, including China, where it offers a vigorous though not always overt competition to Marxism and Leninism for political consciousness. To mention Karl Marx and Nikolai Lenin is to remind us of another, perhaps more surprising version of guardianship, that presented in Lenin's doctrine of the vanguard party with its special knowledge of the laws of history and, as a consequence, its special, indeed its unique, claim to rule. Finally, there is a more obscure instance, one without much influence on the world but interesting because it reveals something of the variety of forms the appeal of guardianship may take. I have in mind the utopia sketched by the illustrious psychologist B. F. Skinner in *Walden Two*.

To Plato, political knowledge constituted the royal science, the supreme art: "No other art or science will have a prior or better right than in the royal science to care for human society and to rule over men in general" (Plato *Dialogues* 276, Jowett trans.). The essence of the art and science of politics is, of course, knowledge of the good of the community, the *polis*. Just as all men are not of equal excellence as physicians or pilots, so some are superior in their knowledge of the political art. And just as excellence as a physician or a pilot requires training, so too men and women must be carefully selected and rigorously trained in order to achieve excellence in the art and science of politics. The guardians must not only, like true philosophers, be completely devoted to the search for truth and, like true philosophers, discern more clearly than all others what is best for the community, but must also be wholly dedicated to achieving that end and therefore must possess no interests of their own inconsistent with the good of the *polis*. Thus they would unite the truth seeking and knowledge of the true philosopher with the dedication of a true king or a true aristocracy — if such could exist — to the good of the community over which they rule.

Obviously rule by philosopher kings would be unlikely to come about by chance. To create such a republic and the class of guardians to rule over it would require exceptional care, including, certainly, much attention to the selection and education of the guardians. Yet if such a republic were to come into existence, its citizens, recognizing the excellence of the rulers and their unswerving commitment to the good of the community, would give to it their support and loyalty. In this sense, in the language not of Plato but of modern democratic ideas, we could say that the government of the guardians would enjoy the consent of the governed.

To leap forward more than two thousand years to the ideas of Lenin is to move into a world, and a view of the world, so different from Plato's that it may seem to be stretching commonalities beyond the breaking point. For an American audience, whatever sympathy for the idea of guardianship that I may have gained by describing the ancient and unthreatening vision of Plato may automatically turn to hostility at the merest association with Leninism. Nonetheless I am convinced that the powerful influence in this century of the ideas described below depends in no small measure on the perennial appeal of the idea of guardianship. Even if the Leninist incarnation of that idea were to disappear, and there is no convincing evidence of that happening, I believe that the idea would — and surely will — reappear in a new incarnation, one that could be far more attractive to people who reject its embodiment in Leninism.

Lenin originally formulated his view, in the essay *What Is To Be Done?*, as an argument for a new kind of revolutionary party. The argument could be and was transposed, however, to the postrevolutionary society the party was instrumental in bringing about. It was then more fully developed in the work of the Hungarian philosopher and literary critic George Lukács, and can be found even in quite recent work, like that of the Mexican Marxist Adolfo Sánchez Vásquez.[3] A synthesis of their views would be something like the following:

The working class occupies a unique historical position, for its liberation necessarily means the inauguration of a society without class divisions based on the ownership or non-ownership of the means of production. In a classless society (in this sense) where the means of production are socially owned and controlled, everyone will be relieved of the burden of economic exploitation and oppression and will enjoy a degree of freedom and opportunities for personal development beyond all previous historical possibility. However, it would be wholly unrealistic to think that a working class shaped by exploitation, oppression, and the dominant culture of capitalism could sufficiently understand its own needs, interests, and potentialities, and the strategies its liberation would require, to bring about, unaided, a revolutionary transformation of capitalism to socialism and the later stage of communism in which the state itself, and with it all forms of collective coercion, will have disappeared. What is needed, then, is a dedicated, incorruptible, and organized group of revolutionaries, a vanguard, who possess the knowledge and the commitment necessary to that task. These revolutionaries would need knowledge of the laws of historical development. That knowledge is to be found in the only body of scientific understanding capable of unlocking the door to liberation: the science of Marxism, now, in virtue of this new insight, the science of Marxism-Leninism. Like Plato's guardians, the members of the vanguard party must be carefully recruited, trained, selected for their dedication to the goal of achieving the liberation of the working class (and thereby humanity itself) and expert in their knowledge of Marxism-Leninism. Since the historical transition may be long and arduous, the leadership of these guardians of the proletariat may well be necessary for some time even after the revolutionary overthrow of the capitalist state. But as with Plato's Guardians, the guiding role of the party would have the consent — if not express, at least implied — of the working class itself, and thus of the overwhelming majority of people.

With B. F. Skinner we turn from contemplative philosophy and revolutionary action to a distinguished modern psychologist renowned for his contributions to learning theory and behavioral psychology, a man with deep faith in rigorous empirical science. In his vision, so far as we can make it out from *Walden Two* and *Beyond Freedom and Dignity*, the guardian's knowledge is the modern psychologist's science of behavior. The philosopher king is replaced by the psychologist king who, like his predecessor in *The Republic*, possesses the scientific knowledge that is necessary and sufficient, it seems, for the fulfillment of human potential. Once a group of human beings had experienced the beneficent rule of such a guardian, they would cease their foolish, vain, and self-defeating efforts to govern themselves, give up the illusions of democracy, and willingly — nay enthusiastically — consent to the gentle and enlightened rule of the psychologist king.

Despite their enormous differences, what is striking about these three visions is how much they have in common. Each in its own way poses an alternative to democracy and challenges the assumption that, at least as we now find them, people are competent to govern themselves. Some of these commonalities are pointed out below. But here consider some assumptions that an advocate of guardianship might share with an advocate of democracy.


## THREE SHARED ASSUMPTIONS

The idea of guardianship is a formidable rival to the democratic process in part, though certainly not wholly, because it begins — or at any rate *can* begin — with some of the same assumptions. First, advocates of guardianship assume, as does everyone who is not a philosophical anarchist, that the good or welfare of some collection of people for which guardianship is proposed — citizens of a city-state, a country, or whatever — requires that they be subject to some binding collective decisions, or laws, that in at least some cases will have to be enforced by a state. In short, advocates of both democracy and guardianship agree, as anarchists do not, on the need for a state.

Second, advocates of guardianship could accept a moral principle fundamental in democratic ideas, that the good or interest of each person who is subject to the laws is entitled to equal consideration. On this assumption, no person is *intrinsically* superior to another, no matter how greatly one may be superior to another in extrinsic or instrumental worth. An advocate of rule by a meritocracy is not bound to accept this basic moral axiom, and no doubt some would reject it, but a meritocrat is not logically required to reject it. On the contrary, one could argue that only a body of highly qualified guardians could reasonably be expected to possess the knowledge and virtue to protect, within the limits of possibility, the good of everyone subject to the state. Indeed, this is exactly what the Guardians in *The Republic* are said to be best qualified to do.

Finally, though this may come as a surprise, the rival ideals both presuppose that the process of governing the state ought to be restricted to those who are qualified to govern. To admit such an assumption may on first appearance seem to constitute a rejection of democracy and to give the game away at the outset to supporters of guardianship. It is true that in democratic theory, philosophy, and argument this dangerous premise is rarely made explicit — precisely, I think, because it is so dangerous. Yet I do not believe that any important political philosopher in the democratic tradition — Locke, Rousseau, Bentham, James Mill, for example — has rejected it, though perhaps only John Stuart Mill made it fully explicit.[4] Both democratic theory and practise have always distinguished in at least two ways between those who are and those who are not qualified to govern. Only members of some specific unit — Athens, the United States, Iceland — are entitled to the rights of citizenship in that unit and thus to participate in governing that unit; those who are not members of the specific unit — Spartans, Canadians, Danes — are not so entitled, though they are entitled to govern their *own* unit.[5] But not *all* members — and this is the more germane point — are admitted to citizenship, because from the very beginning of democratic ideas and institutions, a substantial proportion have always been held to be unqualified: children. That children are denied the rights of full citizenship because they are not qualified shows conclusively, I think, that democratic theory and practise shares with the idea of guardianship an assumption that governing must be restricted to those who are qualified to govern.[6] Participation in governing is not, despite the language of universalism one encounters in Locke, Rousseau, Jefferson, and the Declaration of Independence, a categorical right of all human beings.

Once confronted, this dangerous and yet obvious fact makes it immediately clear that a central issue in the controversy between advocates of democracy and guardianship is whether the good or interests of ordinary folk are best protected by themselves, acting through the democratic process, or by a meritorious elite possessing unusual knowledge and virtue.

## WHAT ARE THE QUALIFICATIONS
## OF THE QUALIFIED?

If advocates of both democracy and guardianship agree (as I have indicated they do) that governing should be restricted to those who are qualified to govern, what do they mean by "qualified"? I think both sides would agree that in order to be qualified to govern—in that sense to be politically competent—people should possess three qualities. They should have an adequate understanding of the proper ends, goals, or objectives that the government should strive to reach. Let me call this the quality of *moral understanding* or *moral capacity.* Since it would be utterly bootless if people only knew these ends but did not act to achieve them, they should also possess a strong disposition actually to seek these ends. This quality may be called by an old name: *virtue.* Moral understanding and virtue in combination make for *moral competence.* But moral competence is not sufficient: we all know what the road to Hell is paved with. Rulers should also know the best, most efficient, or most appropriate means to achieve desirable ends. In short, they ought to possess adequate *technical or instrumental knowledge.*[7]

No single one of these, or even any pair of them, would be sufficient. All three are required. To be properly qualified to govern, one should be both morally competent and instrumentally competent. In combination, then, the three qualities define *political competence.*

Not so fast! one might want to object. If I accept the assumptions so far, one might say, in effect have I not already conceded the case for guardianship? But even if this conclusion were to follow, on what ground could one reasonably reject the premises? Would anyone argue that people who definitely lack political competence—children, for example—are nevertheless entitled to participate fully in governing this country? One must confront the case of children and the reasons for denying them the right to vote. If we agree that they are not qualified—though they may someday become qualified—then no matter how uncomfortable it may make us feel, we have accepted the premise that people who are definitely unqualified should not be permitted to participate fully in governing.

One might concede the point but object that children are a unique category. Yet once one accepts a boundary that excludes some persons, one is obliged to justify drawing the boundary there rather than somewhere else. The exact location of the boundary is surely not self-evident, even among democrats. For example, what are we to say about persons who suffer from such severe mental retardation or insanity that they are legally judged to be incompetent to protect their own fundamental interests and are placed under the control of a legal guardian, a paternalistic authority equivalent to a parent? And what about the troublesome question of whether persons convicted of felonies should be deprived of the right to vote?

Where the boundary that divides political competence from incompetence is to be drawn is the crucial issue. From Plato to the present day, advocates of guardianship have insisted that the average person is not qualified to govern; that the Strong Principle of Equality is an absurdity; that a definitely better qualified minority of adults could be found, or if need be created by education; and that this minority, the potential guardians, ought to rule. To be sure, some advocates would say that their system of guardianship is intended only to be transitional, though in practise the transitional period might prove to be indefinitely stretched out. Lenin appears to have held such a view, as did the Hungarian Marxist Lukács. It is also a normal part of the justification for Latin American military dictatorships, as in the Pinochet regime in Chile. However, the argument for transitional, though possibly quite long lasting, guardianship is in substance very similar to the defense of guardianship as an ideal and more enduring regime. Even Plato assumed that his republic would be subject to inevitable decay, dissolution, and ultimate transformation into a different kind of regime.

Advocates of guardianship set forth both negative and positive reasons for its superiority to democracy. They contend not only that ordinary people can be convincingly shown to lack the necessary qualifications for ruling, but also that a minority — an elite of knowledge and virtue, a "vanguard," an aristocracy in the original and etymological meaning — can be discovered or created. Unlike the great majority of people, this qualified minority would possess both the moral and the instrumental competence needed to justify a claim to govern.

### Moral Competence

To begin with, advocates of guardianship generally contend that people differ greatly in their moral competence, and that only a few can reasonably be expected to possess the moral knowledge and virtue required for rulership. Democrats, in contrast, have generally assumed that an adequate level of moral competence is widely distributed among adult human beings, and that no distinctively superior moral elite can be identified or safely entrusted with the power to rule over the rest. As Garry Wills has shown,[8] Jefferson and the philosophers of the Scottish Enlightenment held that most human beings possess a fundamental sense of right and wrong that is not significantly stronger in some groups than in others. Indeed, in their view, the cowherd might have a clearer judgment on elementary moral issues than the nobleman at court. John Rawls's whole system of justice depends finally on the assumption that human beings are fundamentally equal as "moral persons," that is, in their capacity for arriving at a reasonable conception of what is just.[9] Thus putting aside the stray case of the person who is definitely impaired, every adult of ordinary intelligence is capable of making adequate moral judgments.

But do not views of this kind greatly exaggerate the moral capacity of the average person? In the first place, the meritocrat might object, many people seem to lack much of an understanding of their *own* basic needs, interests, or good. Is it not a fact that very few people bother to reflect very deeply, if at all, as to what would constitute a good life? Are many people given to much introspection? Do many of us ever manage to obtain anything beyond a rather superficial understanding of ourselves? "Know thyself," said the Delphic oracle, and Socrates gave his life to doing so. But few of us live with such devotion to that purpose. To take some examples, the Jewish prophets, Christ, the ancient Hindu texts, Buddha, even so modern a philosopher as Bertrand Russell, all have deplored the utter futility of searching for happiness through the endless gratification of desire, particularly through the acquisition and consumption of things. Yet have not we Americans made the consumption of a never-ending and forever increasing stream of material goods a principle objective of our lives and organized our society toward that end? And does not most of the world nowadays, whether Hindu, Buddhist, Jewish, Christian, or Marxist, rush headlong toward the same goal? Or consider this: for three centuries we Americans avidly collaborated in the destruction of our natural environment, indifferent in the main to its importance to our well-being, a conclusion that a little introspection would have revealed to a great many people, as it did to a few.

One could multiply the examples. Well, then, our meritocrat asks, can you deny that a great many people — not children but adults — are unable or unwilling to do whatever may be necessary to acquire an elementary understanding of their own needs, their own interests, their own good? If they do not even understand their own interests, are they not, like children, incompetent to govern themselves — let alone others?

What is more, our meritocrat will no doubt say, most people find it difficult, perhaps even impossible, to take the good of others — very many others, anyway — into account in making decisions. Their deficiency is partly one of knowledge, partly one of virtue. If it is often difficult in a very complex world to know enough to judge accurately where one's own interests lie, it is infinitely more daunting to acquire an adequate understanding of the good of other people in one's society, people whom one does not know and could only know about indirectly. The information costs are far too high for most people to bear, and it is downright inhuman to ask them to do so.

Even more to the point, the meritocrat continues, most people seem unwilling to assign anything like an equal weight to the interests of a stranger or an unknown if those interests conflict with one's own interests or the interests of one's family or immediate circle. Yet even in a small country, and all the more so in a country as large as the United States, most others exist outside one's intimate circle of family and friends or the broader circle of acquaintances. In this sense, most people are egoists, not altruists.[10] But individual egoism is inconsistent with the need for virtue as a qualification for ruling. In democratic orders, our meritocrat might continue, individual and group interests will usually prevail over general interests or the public good. To take an extreme example, where egoism prevails who will protect the interests of future generations, including their interest in living in a world that has not been made a hideous nightmare by the aftermath of a nuclear war?[11]

If both knowledge and virtue are required for moral competence, and moral competence is required for political competence, can we really conclude that very many people are politically competent — that is, qualified to govern?

## Technical Competence

If it is problematic, to say the least, whether very many people possess the moral qualifications for ruling, their lack of technical competence with respect to nuclear weapons and strategy is not problematic at all. Yet most of the debate on this issue is not ostensibly about moral ends, it is about technical means to these ends. Nor can we say that the problem of nuclear weapons is unique, or for that matter exceptional. Extreme, yes, but not exceptional. As was pointed out in the introduction, most public policy questions these days involve highly technical issues: not only questions of obvious technicality like nuclear waste disposal or the regulation of recombinant DNA research, for example, but even matters closer to everyday life — health care and delivery, social security, unemployment, inflation, tax reform, crime.

We who are not experts on these matters could deal with them more intelligently if the experts agreed on technical solutions, or, failing that, if we could judge the comparative expertise of the experts. But experts do not agree and we do not know how to evaluate the qualifications of the experts.


## The Need for Specialization

These deficiencies in the moral and instrumental competence of ordinary people can only be overcome, Plato argued twenty five centuries ago, by specializing to a degree that most people can hardly be expected to do. Even if most persons were potentially capable of acquiring the qualifications desirable for ruling, they would lack the time to do so. A society, after all, needs many different kinds of activities. Ruling is only one activity. We also need plumbers, carpenters, machinists, doctors, teachers, physicists, mathematicians, painters, dancers, and in a modern society thousands upon thousands of other specialists far more various than anything Plato could have imagined. Acquiring the skills necessary to these tasks and then performing them makes it impossible for very many people to spend the time needed to gain the moral and instrumental competence for ruling. As I have already indicated, the art and science of ruling is difficult; in a world as complex as ours, extraordinarily difficult: it is probably easier to become an excellent mathematician than to become an excellent ruler. To suppose that many people have the capacity to acquire and use well a great number of specialized skills is merely romantic. True polymaths are a rarity. Would you entrust yourself to a physician who was also attempting seriously to be a ballet dancer, an opera singer, an architect, an accountant, and a stockbroker?

So it is, then, that in a well ordered society just as some persons would receive the rigorous training and meritocratic selection essential to the art and science of the physician, so also would others be rigorously trained and selected to function well as rulers. Given the crucial function of rulership, nothing could be of greater importance than the education of our rulers, whether they be ordinary citizens in a democracy or specialized leaders in a system of meritocratic rule. And just as democratic philosophers have always stressed the importance of educating citizens for citizenship in a democratic order, so in the political philosophy of guardianship, much attention is devoted, as it is by Plato in *The Republic*, to the selection and training of the guardians.


## HISTORICAL EXPERIENCE

The idea of guardianship might be fine as a utopian fancy, one may reply, but applying it to the real world is something else again. Do we have any reason for thinking that the ideal of guardianship has any practical relevance?

I have already said that the ideal has often been badly misused to justify an evil or incompetent authoritarian regime. Even the most vicious and oppressive monarchies, oligarchies, and dictatorships have tried to present themselves as the true guardians of the collective interest. Yet all political ideals have been greatly abused. It would be a mistake to judge the possibilities of an ideal only by the worst cases. We should also consider the best cases.

Of these, perhaps the most impressive is the Republic of Venice, which endured, though of course not unchanged, for about eight centuries — for sheer endurance something worthy of the *Guinness Book of World Records*. But it not only endured. As regimes go in the history of mankind, it has to be counted as exceptionally successful. Although it had its faults, on the whole it provided peace and prosperity to its citizens, had an excellent legal system, possessed an elaborate, carefully constructed, and closely observed constitution, was a center dazzling in its creativity in the arts, architecture, town planning, and music, suffered comparatively little from outbreaks of popular discontent, and appears by and large to have enjoyed widespread legitimacy among the Venetian people. Yet from about 1300 onward it was legally governed by less than two thousand citizens, about two percent of the republic's population. Although its rulers were not selected and trained in the rigorous fashion prescribed in *The Republic*, every male member of one of the aristocratic families entitled to participate in the government of the republic would have known from infancy that to participate in governing Venice was to be his privilege and responsibility. The constitutional system was carefully constructed to insure that the officials, and particularly the doge, would act not from self-interested motives of personal or family aggrandizement but to secure the broader interests of the republic.

One could cite other examples, such as the Republic of Florence under the Medici in the fifteenth century, or even China during periods of stability and prosperity under the rule of an emperor and a bureaucracy greatly influenced by Confucian ideas of meritocratic rule.

So it would be a mistake to say that the ideal of guardianship is impossible of fulfillment in at least a reasonably satisfactory approximation.

## CONCLUSION

In contrast to the democratic vision, then, there is another: a vision of a well-qualified minority, the guardians or experts, who rule over the rest, governing in the best interests of all, fully respecting the principle of equal consideration, indeed perhaps upholding it far better than would the people if they were to govern themselves. Paradoxically, then, at its best such a system might actually rest on the consent of all. In this way, a system of guard-

ianship might attain one of the most important ends of both anarchism and democracy — but by very different means.

It is a powerful vision. It has always been the strongest com-
petitor to the democratic vision, and remains so today, when so
many regimes — left, right, revolutionary, conservative, traditional
— justify themselves by appealing to it for legitimacy. If democracy were to decline and perhaps even disappear from human history in the centuries to come, I think its place would be taken by
regimes based on the vision of government by guardians of virtue
and knowledge.

# 3

# A Critique of Guardianship

HE CONTROL OF NUCLEAR WEAPONS offers a way of testing out the claims for guardianship. For one thing, the opportunities for exercising control over some of the most crucial decisions seem to be inherently limited to so few persons that controlling them democratically is simply out of the question.

To take one of the most horrifying of all possibilities, the decision whether or not to launch nuclear weapons rests solely with the president. It is surely not an exaggeration to say that no single person has ever before been given such an incredible concentration of authority over such a consequential matter. In actuality, the situation is rather more complicated. There are grounds for thinking that presidents may secretly delegate to military commanders their authority to launch in the event that the president himself is incapacitated — incinerated might be the proper word — in an enemy attack. Eisenhower, Kennedy, and Johnson seem to have done so, and one supposes that their successors followed the same practice.[1] In addition, the commander-in-chief of the Strategic Air Command (SAC) is authorized to launch the nuclear bomber force in order to protect it from what is judged to be an incoming missile attack. The bomber force then proceeds to holding positions for further orders, presumably from the president or in some circumstances the SAC commander. All these arrangements depend, of course, on the preservation of command systems.

But centralized command and control structures would probably be so damaged by a nuclear attack that decisions to launch would be made by individual commanders—of bombers and submarines, for example—with little or no knowledge of the overall picture.[2]

The upshot is, then, that decisions quite likely of greater importance than any in the previous history of mankind can legally be made by a single person, the president, or at the outside—an even more appalling possibility—by almost any of the twenty five thousand persons scattered over the world who are involved in the nuclear command and controls system.[3]

The decision (or decisions) to launch nuclear weapons should of course be distinguished from decisions about the *policies* intended to guide or determine a decision to launch them. A decision to launch entails a substantial element of discretionary judgment that is probably irreducible and unavoidable. To this extent we are all inescapably dependent for our existence on our *de facto* guardians. But a decision as to whether or not nuclear weapons should be employed in a concrete instance, and how they are to be used—what sorts of targets should or should not be selected, for example—could and should be strongly influenced, at least in principle, by established policy. No one, so far as I am aware, seriously contests this principle. The question is the extent to which these policies can and should be made by democratic processes.

For reasons discussed in the first chapter, from the decision to use nuclear weapons against Japan in 1945 down to the present, most of the crucial choices about nuclear weapons strategy have been made by a very small group of decision makers whose decisions, including those of the president, have been subject only weakly, if at all, to democratic procedures. I shall describe some of the alternatives at stake in their decisions in a moment. The important point is that for the better part of four decades these questions were not even subjected to political debate, much less to control by public opinion expressed through elections and congressional action. For all practical purposes, on these matters *no public opinion existed and the democratic process was inoperable.*

Whether we like it or not, then, unless we can discover radically different ways of exercising control over such decisions, it looks to be the case that democratic control is simply not feasible. Failing hitherto undiscovered solutions, the alternatives, in Aristotle's terms, are either monarchy or tyranny, or at most either aristocracy or oligarchy, but not either a balanced polity or democracy. If this turns out to be the case, would we not want our *de facto* guardians to possess the qualities of ideal guardians: knowledge and virtue?

It is arguable that even as things stand, the scientific, military, and managerial experts involved in nuclear weapons control and command do have these qualities, not to perfection, of course, but within human limits to a satisfactory degree. I should not be surprised if many people in the nuclear weapons command and control system believe this to be so. If pressed they might say something like this:

Obviously we possess superior instrumental knowledge. If only because of secrecy and our occupational and professional specialization in this incredibly complicated field, our knowledge must be far better than people outside the system can hope to acquire. As to moral knowledge, as Americans and human beings we certainly share the dominant values on which there is widespread consensus in the United States: the desirability of surviving as a nation, for example, and the horror of a full scale nuclear war. Finally, as to virtue, can we not be firmly counted on to act in behalf of the common good? Since every person in the command system, from the president on down, will probably be a prime target, our individual interests become utterly irrelevant in thinking about nuclear war. Nothing concentrates one's mind more powerfully on the task of balancing the survival of the nation against the risks of nuclear extinction than the knowledge that oneself, one's family, and all that one holds dear will surely perish in the holocaust.

So let us examine the claims for guardianship against the experience with the control of nuclear forces.

## NUCLEAR WEAPONS POLICIES:
## FIVE MORAL QUESTIONS

As I have already suggested, decisions about nuclear forces are not merely instrumental. They also involve moral choices, some of which are extraordinarily difficult and perplexing. An important contribution of the 1983 pastoral letter of the American Catholic bishops was to bring these moral issues to public attention and thereby to stimulate thinking and discussion by many citizens who had never before given them serious thought. Although the pastoral letter was criticized, even its severest critics did not deny the bishops' assumption that decisions about nuclear weapons require both instrumental and moral judgments. Let me therefore mention some of the moral questions brought out in the pastoral letter and the discussion it provoked.[4]

## Is Nuclear War Morally Justifiable?

At the outset, we confront the question whether nuclear weapons should ever be used in an all-out attack or counterattack. It is one of the tragic ironies of nuclear weapons that almost everyone believes that a full-scale nuclear war would destroy the contestants, and with them much of civilization. As early as 1956, President Eisenhower foresaw that such a time was rapidly approaching. In a "personal and confidential" letter to a publisher, he wrote:

> I have spent my life in the study of military strength as a deterrent to war, and in the character of military armaments necessary to win a war. The study of the first of these questions is still profitable, but we are rapidly approaching the point that no war can be won. War implies a contest; when you get to the point that contest is no longer involved and the outlook comes close to destruction of the enemy and suicide for ourselves — an outlook that neither side can ignore — then arguments as to the exact amount of available strength as compared to somebody else's are no longer the vital issues. When we get to the point, as we one day will, that both sides know that in any outbreak of general hostilities, regardless of the element of surprise, destruction will be both reciprocal and complete, possibly we will have sense enough to meet at the conference table with the understanding that the era of armaments has ended and the human race must conform its actions to this truth or die.[5]

A decision to undertake a nuclear war, or to prepare for that possibility, therefore depends only to a small degree on instrumental judgments, for what it entails above all else is a moral judgment. On the moral impermissibility of starting a nuclear war, the judgment of the Catholic bishops is absolute and unequivocal: "We do not perceive any situation in which the deliberate initiation of nuclear war on however restricted a scale can be morally justified."[6]

But if it would be morally monstrous to launch a nuclear war, is it also wrong to risk that possibility? How great a risk, if any, is morally permissible? Although the bishops evidently struggled with this question, their answer is less clear-cut. For, like most people who have given long and hard thought to the problem of avoiding war, they were aware that risking nuclear war is the essence of deterrence, and deterrence looks to be the only realistic alternative to surrender.

### Is Deterrence Permissible?

The paradox of deterrence is well understood by its advocates: to avoid a morally impermissible war, each side must make the other believe that it will, if attacked, fight such a war. In the letter quoted above Eisenhower wrote: "[A]lready we have come to the point where safety cannot be assumed by arms alone. But I repeat that their usefulness becomes concentrated more and more in their characteristics as deterrents than in instruments with which to obtain victory over opponents as in 1945. In this regard, today we are further separated from the end of World War II than the beginning of the century was separated from the beginning of the sixteenth century."

Moral theory and theology generally recognize that ends may conflict and thus gains for one end may have to be balanced against damage to another. But they have a hard time specifying the trade off that would be morally acceptable, and even more difficulty with the evaluation of risk. Yet risk is at the heart of deterrence. Some opponents of deterrence argue, in effect, that the costs of nuclear war to human (and some would say, divine) ends are so vast that *no risk* of their use is morally justified.[7] To avoid that risk, some opponents of deterrence would say, we should unilaterally destroy our nuclear stockpile. To this, advocates of deterrence reply that the process of unilateral disarmament would itself engender great instability and the risk of war. Moreover, *some* risk is justifiable as the only way to prevent the well-nigh inevitable outcome of unilateral disarmament, surrender to the Soviet Union and their unending domination.[8]

I want to call your attention to two aspects of this controversy over deterrence. First, notice that a rational — or merely reasonable — judgment on the issue does not entirely depend, perhaps mainly does not depend, on instrumental or empirical questions but also requires a moral assessment. Second, notice how complexly intertwined the moral and empirical issues are. Theories of rational decision tell us that a judgment as to whether a given risk is acceptable depends on one's judgments as to the costs and gains of alternative outcomes, the probability of each outcome, and one's attitude toward risk taking itself — whether, for example, one prefers to go after the best possible outcome or to avoid the worst possible outcome. Now it is one thing to play games with strategies when the parameters can be neatly specified and quite another when almost nothing can be. In the end, even expert judgments necessarily turn less on superior instrumental information or empirical knowledge than on hunches, intuitions — including moral intuitions — and feelings.

### In What Circumstances, if Ever, Should Nuclear Weapons Be Used?

If a full scale nuclear war is suicidal, are there any circumstances short of nuclear war in which the use of nuclear weapons is justified? Although pacifists would of course say no, and many other opponents of deterrence would agree with them on this point, unless one takes an absolute pacifist position the moral issues are complex. One who believes, as most people do, that in some circumstances waging war is morally justified, must consider what circumstances, if any, would justify the use of nuclear weapons.

Here too the pastoral letter is germane to our inquiry because the doctrine of just war in Catholic theology compelled the bishops to confront the question. Although I shall not try to summarize that doctrine or the bishops' argument, let me mention a few aspects of both. Among the criteria for a just war are the probability of success, "a difficult criterion to apply, but its purpose is to prevent irrational resort to force or hopeless resistance when the outcome of either will clearly be disproportionate or futile"; the need for proportionality: "the damage to be inflicted and the costs incurred by war must be proportionate to the good expected in taking up arms"; and *jus in bello,* the principle that the conduct of war must be scrutinized for its adherence to proportionality and to the principle of discrimination, which "prohibits directly intended attacks on non-combatants and non-military targets."[9]

One does not have to be a Catholic theologian to see that criteria like these make moral sense. However, in conjunction with the moral insanity of an all-out nuclear war, they give rise at once to a number of other questions. For example, if war were to break out would it be justifiable to be the first to use nuclear weapons? The answer depends mainly on an empirical judgment, an estimate of risks and probabilities. If you believe that any use of nuclear weapons stands a very good chance of taking the combatants across a critical and essentially irreversible threshold to general use, and if you believe that all-out nuclear war is morally unjustifiable, then you will conclude that first use is an impermissible strategy. Notice that because a judgment requires an estimate of risk, we are again in a murky zone of empirical and moral judgments.

Or another, more horrifying question: If the Soviet Union were to launch its nuclear missiles against the United States, should we retaliate by launching our missiles against them? A simple knee-jerk reaction is to say yes. But a thoughtful person is likely to ask: to what end? Simply out of revenge? The Catholic bishops say no:

> Retaliatory action, whether nuclear or conventional, which would indiscriminately take many wholly innocent lives, lives of people who are in no way responsible for reckless actions of their government, must also be condemned. This condemnation, in our judgment, applies even to the retaliatory use of weapons strik-

ing enemy cities after our own have already been struck. No Christian can rightfully carry out orders or policies deliberately aimed at killing non-combatants.[10]

## What Targets Are Morally Permissible?

Then there is the dreadful question of target selection, a task that invites us to engage in thinking about the morally unthinkable. To put the awful possibilities in an order that seems to reflect an increasing violation of our moral sensibilities, nuclear weapons could be used against:

- Military forces, including
  - ground forces, and
  - launching sites
- Command and control centers
- Industry, transportation, and other economic centers
- Cities, population centers

In actuality, however, these distinctions are highly artificial. We are not dealing here with daylight precision bombing by American B-52s in World War II but rather Dresden, Tokyo, Hiroshima, and Nagasaki increased by many orders of magnitude. Even an attack against military targets would kill millions of civilians. In war games conducted by the German defense ministry in 1962, 10 to 15 million people theoretically were killed, even though purely military targets had been chosen.[11] The most vital center of Soviet command and control is, of course, the city of Moscow itself. Economic targets are inescapably civilian targets. Despite the learned distinction employed by the nuclear *cognoscenti* between "counterforce" (military targets) and "countervalue" (people), counterforce necessarily entails countervalue.[12]

That it is wrong to kill innocent people and an abomination to kill them indiscriminately and massively is more than an inference from the doctrine of just war employed by the bishops. It is, I should think, a tenet of every religion, every moral system, and every civilized person.[13] Any decision about nuclear targeting is therefore fraught with the most fundamental problems of moral judgment.

## When, if Ever, Would It Be Right to Yield?

If these questions compel one to explore a world of nightmarish possibilities that lie at the outer edge of our capacity for moral judgment, if not indeed beyond it, their impetus carries us toward a zone of possibilities that fear and taboo make it all but impossible to discuss. Yet I shall now enter this forbidden zone by asking at what point, if ever, defeat and surrender would be better than war or the continuation of war.

How to terminate a war is not a popular subject, even among social scientists, as one of them at the Rand Corporation discovered when he attempted to take up this taboo subject some years ago. How a nuclear war, once begun, could be ended is an important and frightening subject, but it remains undiscussed. As Paul Bracken remarks: "Although a few analyses of strategic war terminations have been written, to my knowledge none has ever dealt with war termination in Europe. The lack of attention given to this subject is stunning."[14]

If Bracken's judgment is correct, as I think it is, that command and control would be in disarray, then as a practical matter it might be impossible to terminate hostilities by deliberate choice. He presents the hair-raising prospect of a nuclear war in Europe cascading out of control:

> . . . the sure knowledge that a man's children have been incinerated would be a much stronger pressure for loss of control, especially under circumstances of ambiguous command. Whether it be a German QRA (Quick Reaction Alert Aircraft) pilot with a one-megaton bomb capable of reaching Leningrad, or a Soviet submarine crew informed that Murmansk, and hence their families, had been wiped out, one cannot expect of them a reluctance to launch weapons; revenge would be a powerful incentive to do so. If there is an ambiguous or even a rumored delegation of authority, the likelihood of a frenzied orgy of pulling every trigger possible should not be discounted.[15]

If we were to assume that the problem of command and control could be solved, we must still consider whether a stage might not be quickly reached at which efforts should be made to end a war, without victory and after suffering great damage. If we assume instead that the problem is not likely to be solved, then we have to consider whether the following may not be correct: all-out nuclear war simply cannot be justified, while the probability is low that nuclear war can actually be limited to justifiable levels. But if our nuclear weapons can never be used, then should we not renounce their use and abandon them, if need be unilaterally? The pacifist has no difficulty answering yes, nor would anyone who believes either that Soviet domination would not result, or, if it did, it would not prove to be morally repulsive. To anyone who believes that the result would be Soviet domination and that domination by the Soviets would be morally repulsive, the answer, though less clear cut, is usually the strategy of deterrence. This, as we saw, was the bishop's choice.[16] It is also the choice of most scholars and strategists who have thought about the question, and of most American citizens as well.

## WOULD GUARDIANS KNOW BETTER?

When we reflect on the answers we might give to these five questions — and others we might wish to ask — it becomes obvious that choosing policies concerning nuclear forces unavoidably depends on complex and difficult moral judgments. Yet we have not the slightest reason for supposing that the small circle of policy makers who have established our nuclear policies are particularly well qualified in their moral understanding. Their specialization is, after all, of a very different kind and may, if anything, blunt rather than sharpen their moral sensibilities. Indeed, in the area of nuclear weapons and their use, policy makers may well find the moral issues so deeply disturbing that they avoid discussing them altogether — and may even avoid thinking about them. Bracken's comments are not exactly encouraging:

> There is a pervasive sense among both critics of nuclear weapons and strategists inside the security establishment that questions

of how nuclear weapons would really be used are of irremediable insanity. What passes for a strategic debate is little more
than construction of a facade of nuclear logic to permit getting
on with the day-to-day job of deterrence. The most that can be
said for this practise is that creating a veneer of rationality in
the discussion of nuclear strategy is a ritual used to convince opponents that we are serious about deterrence. In many instances
their motivation is harder to identify, serving only as a psychological defense mechanism against what is, at bottom, an issue
of madness.[17]

An advocate of guardianship might reply: But of course our
*de facto* guardians are not real Guardians in Plato's sense, and that
is precisely the problem. We need to unite moral understanding
with the instrumental knowledge and virtue required for true
guardianship. Under those conditions we could more safely entrust our fate to our rulers.

But I think this reply would be mistaken. To understand why
it is mistaken, we need to consider the other requirements for true
guardianship.


## INSTRUMENTAL KNOWLEDGE

Although moral judgments are always necessary to intelligent decisions, as they obviously are with decisions about nuclear forces,
they are never sufficient. One must also make judgments about
the empirical world, how it operates, what feasible alternatives
it allows, the probable consequences of each, and so on. At least
some of these judgments require specialized knowledge, of a sort
we cannot reasonably expect most people to possess, what has here
been called instrumental knowledge. If nuclear weapons policy
is perhaps unrepresentative in the extreme difficulty of its moral
choices, it is perhaps less atypical in its requirements for technical
knowledge, for these, though severe, may be no more severe than
for many other complex issues.

Because both moral understanding and instrumental knowledge are always necessary for policy judgments, neither alone can
ever be sufficient. It is precisely here that any argument for rule

by a purely technocratic elite must fail. As has just been seen in the case of nuclear forces, technocrats are no more qualified than others to make the essential moral judgments, and they may be less so.

But technocrats also suffer from at least three other defects that look to be irremediable in a world where knowledge is as complex as it is in ours. In the first place, the specialization required in order to acquire a high degree of expert knowledge is today inherently limiting: one becomes a specialist in *something*, that is, in *one* thing, and by necessity remains ignorant of other things.

Second, Plato's royal science simply does not exist, and therefore its practitioners cannot exist. Thus, *pace* Plato, there is no single art or science that can satisfactorily demonstrate a claim to unite in itself the moral and instrumental understanding required for intelligent policy making in today's world. Perhaps a few philosophers, social scientists, or even natural scientists might make such an extravagant claim for their own specialty. But the weakness of any such claims could easily be shown to the satisfaction of most of us by a simple test: let them explain what their policies would be in a dozen different areas of policy, let them be subjected to examination by experts in each area, and let us be the judges of their performance.

The third weakness of technocrats as policy makers is that on a great many questions of policy, instrumental judgments depend on assumptions that are not strictly technical, scientific, or even very rigorous. Often these assumptions reflect a kind of ontological judgment: the world is this way, not that, it tends to work this way, not that. With nuclear weapons, for example, ordinary people, as Bracken points out, are likely to believe in Murphy's famous law. They believe that if things can go wrong, they probably will go wrong. Although supported by a great deal of experience, in fact probably as well supported by experience as most generalizations in the social sciences, Murphy's law is of course not a well validated empirical law in the strict sense. It is a common sense judgment about a tendency of things, an ontological view about the nature of the world.

Because of these defects in specialized knowledge, experts often utterly fail to comprehend how the real world may stubbornly refuse to play by their rules.[18] Although the gaffes of specialists in nuclear weapons planning tend to be hidden from public view, and may never be known until it is too late, enough is known to indicate that specialists in nuclear weapons are no exception to the general experience.

Thus the decision to increase the destructive power of launchers by adding multiple, independently targeted re-entry vehicles (MIRVs) carrying nuclear warheads is now understood to have been a mistake. The Russians naturally undertook to deploy MIRVs on their launchers, and the problem of arms control has become even more difficult. The Pentagon now suggests that perhaps the launchers armed with MIRVs should be replaced on both sides by smaller launchers each carrying a single warhead, thus making verification easier. Yet at the time the MIRV decision was made, many critics, arguing from a common sense point of view — and a certain ontological judgment about the way the world works — contended that what has happened would surely happen. Nor is one's confidence in the implicit assumptions of decision-makers much strengthened by knowing that as late as 1982, the North American Aerospace Defense Command (NORAD) warning center lacked a reliable emergency power supply. Somehow that simple problem had "just slipped through the cracks."[19] Or consider the case of the Football, a fit subject for black humor. The Football, or Black Bag, is a locked briefcase with coded messages that the president would use to command the military to launch the nuclear forces and that is meant always to be immediately at hand for the president's use. However, an official who had been in charge of the Football from Johnson's administration through Carter's later wrote:

> No new President in my time ever had more than one briefing on the contents of the Football, and that was before each one took office, when it was one briefing among dozens. Not one president, to my knowledge, and I know because it was in my care, ever got an update on the contents of the Football, although material in it changed constantly. Not one president could open the Football — only the warrant officers, the military aides and the Director of the Military Office have the combination. If the guy with the Football has a heart attack or got shot on the way to the President, they'd have to blow the goddamn thing open.[20]

Experience with nuclear weapons decisions thus appears to lend further support to the conclusion of common sense that technocrats ought to be ruled over, not rulers. This conclusion is summed up in Clemenceau's famous aphorism that war is too important to be left to the generals, a principle amply justified by the slaughter that highly trained general staffs managed to bring about during the First World War. Human experience, codified in Clemenceau's comment and Murphy's law, provides little ground for counting on experts to possess the wisdom to rule that is promised by the theory of guardianship.[21]

### Risk, Uncertainty, and Trade Offs

Although these defects in the judgments of experts on questions of public policy have frequently been observed, recent analyses of decision making have brought to light a new and fatal flaw in the argument for guardianship that older philosophical defense and criticism were not equipped to discern. The defense of guardianship often presupposes that moral and scientific knowledge, and thus political judgments, can be based on rational certainty. Thus in comparison with the judgments of ordinary people, which reflect all the uncertainties of mere opinion, the guardians can acquire knowledge of what is best for the community that approaches something like rational certainty. Yet any assumption of this kind neglects an inherent characteristic of judgments about most important issues of policy: that they must be based on assessments of *risk, uncertainty,* and *trade offs.*

Policy decisions are almost always risky at best, in the sense that they require a choice between alternatives the consequences of which are only probable. If the consequences were certain, some of the anguish of decision making would vanish. But what is so dismaying is the terrible riskiness of the outcomes. Suppose one faces the following situation. An unusual and virulent form of influenza has appeared in Asia, and it is expected to reach the United States. Unless a program is adopted to attack it, the disease will kill 600 people. Two alternative programs have been proposed. If one is adopted, 200 people will be saved. If the other is adopted, there is a one-third probability that 600 people will be saved, and a two-third probability that no one will be saved.

Not only is there no unambiguously right answer to this problem, but it has been found experimentally that when the alternatives are formulated in the way just given, most people will choose the first alternative. Yet with a different — though logically identical — formulation, most people will choose the second alternative! Moreover, this reversal "is as common among sophisticated respondents as among naive ones." In the face of risks or choices, people commonly make logically inconsistent judgments — and the performance of experts, it appears, is no better than that of ordinary people.[22]

However, the problem of rational choice is made even more difficult because — unlike the example just given — ordinarily the probabilities themselves are unknown. The outcomes are not merely risky in a probabilistic sense: they are genuinely uncertain in the sense that we can at best only guess at probabilities over a large, vague range.

At the same time, virtually all important policy decisions require a judgment about the relative trade offs between different values: equality versus liberty, high wages versus international competitiveness, savings versus consumption, short-run gains versus long-run gains, and so on.

Ordinarily, policy judgments require an assessment of both uncertainties and trade offs. When these are combined, the superior competence of experts diminishes to the vanishing point. For example, suppose we could choose between two strategies. One carries a substantial chance that nuclear war can be indefinitely avoided; but if it does occur, virtually the entire population of the United States will be wiped out. The other strategy stands considerably less chance of avoiding war, but a war is likely to cause fewer deaths — perhaps around a quarter of the U. S. population. Clearly there are not, nor can there be, "expert" answers to problems like these.

## VIRTUE

*Knowledge*, whether moral, instrumental, or practical, is not the only problem. There is also the question whether our putative guardians could be trusted to *seek* the general good rather than merely their own: whether they would possess in adequate measure the quality here called virtue.

The question raised by the argument for guardianship is not whether *delegated* authority might be abused. The issue is not, for example, whether a very small number of American officials making decisions about nuclear weapons — officials who are formally and to some extent actually subject to political controls, who were themselves reared in the American political culture with its emphasis on democratic values, and who for many reasons may be sensitive to public opinion — might misuse their authority. That the abuse of delegated authority is a serious problem in democratic orders, no one, I imagine, would deny. But the issue here is something else. The theory of guardianship, after all, does not propose that we should delegate some authority to rulers; it does not even propose that we should delegate all authority to rulers. For their authority would not be *delegated* at all, at least in any sense of the term that would have meaning to a democrat. In effect, all authority to rule is permanently *alienated*, not delegated; the people cannot legally or constitutionally, or I suppose rationally or morally, recover authority whenever they think it desirable to do so. Their only recourse is revolution.

Not only would the guardians be free of popular controls, however defective these are at times in democratic orders. Presumably they would also not hold democratic values, and no doubt would have only contempt for public *opinion* as not true *knowledge*.

Having mentioned Clemenceau's aphorism and Murphy's law, perhaps I should add two others. The third, which is perhaps even more well known, and equally well if not better supported by human experience, is Lord Acton's assertion that power tends to corrupt, and absolute power corrupts absolutely. The fourth is John Stuart Mill's: "The rights and interests of every or any person are only secure from being disregarded when the person interested is himself able, and habitually disposed, to stand up for them. . . . [H]uman beings are only secure from evil at the hands of others in proportion as they have the power of being, and are, self-*protecting*."[23]

The generalizations of Mill and Acton, like those of Clemenceau and the apocryphal Murphy, are not really "laws," of course, in the hard-edged sense. They are, rather, practical judgments, prudential rules, informed conclusions about the ways of the world. But anyone who believes them to be roughly right as descriptions of the world, as I do, will find little appeal in the vision of guardianship.

## HISTORICAL EXPERIENCE

This judgment is buttressed, I think, by recent historical experience. The conditions that made the Republic of Venice possible no longer exist and are unlikely to reappear in this century or the next. In our age we have witnessed a new historical phenomenon, which we have called totalitarianism. While the novel and extreme characteristics of those regimes have often been exaggerated, they have greatly sharpened our awareness of the vast potentialities for misrule contained in modern society. Throughout the world, authoritarian regimes varying greatly in structure, ideology, and performance have all laid claim to legitimacy as the true and only guardians of the general good. Their record justifies at least three conclusions.

First, the essential truth in Acton's melancholy aphorism has been reaffirmed. Second, we observe in these systems a strong propensity for blunder, because the power of the rulers leads to a tendency for information to be distorted by those who report to them and by the unchecked eccentricities of the rulers themselves. Third, none has developed a satisfactory way of identifying, recruiting, and training the guardians for their responsibilities, or for removing guardians at the highest level who are unsatisfactory. Thus these regimes lack, and conspicuously lack, rulers who possess the virtue and the knowledge, moral, instrumental, and practical, required to justify their power as guardians.

## WHY WE SHOULD REJECT THE IDEA
## OF PHILOSOPHERS AS KINGS – AND VICE VERSA

Prudence and practical wisdom therefore counsel us to reject as illusory the hope that the best possible regime will be attained only when "philosophers are kings, or the kings and princes of this world have the spirit and power of philosophy, and political greatness and wisdom meet in one, and those commoner natures who pursue one to the exclusion of the other are compelled to stand aside." (*The Republic* 474, Jowett trans.).

For the two activities exclude one another. I do not mean that rulers cannot have a somewhat "philosophic" cast of mind, as some have had. But to have a philosophic cast of mind is one thing, to be a philosopher is another. By philosopher I do not mean the word in its present-day professional sense, as one who teaches in an academic department of philosophy, writes in journals of philosophy, and so on. I mean it in the sense of Socrates and Plato, as one engaged in a passionate search for truth, enlightenment, and understanding, particularly perhaps about justice and human good. Rulers are unlikely to have much interest in such a search, and few would find the results comforting. Nor can philosophers in Plato's sense have much desire to rule, for it will impede their search for truth, as they well know. Plato himself was well aware of this, and some scholars have argued that *The Republic* is ironic: Plato means for us to understand why it is impossible. However that may be, in his famous metaphor of the cave he tells us that one who leaves the cave with its images flickering on the wall from the light of a distant fire, and sees what is real and true under the full light of the sun, will be reluctant to return to the cave. But the world of politics is in the cave, where truth is never wholly accessible.

Prudence and practical wisdom will argue against the vision of guardianship on yet other grounds. An imperfect democracy is a misfortune for its people, but an imperfect authoritarian regime is an abomination. If prudence counsels a maximin strategy — choose the alternative that is the best of the worst outcomes — then the experience of the twentieth century tells powerfully against the idea of guardianship.

But a *maximizing* strategy will, I believe, also lead us to endorse democracy rather than guardianship. For in its ideal outcomes, democracy is better. In an ideal system of guardianship, only the guardians can exercise one of the most fundamental of all freedoms, the freedom to participate in the making of the laws that will be binding on oneself and one's community. But in an ideal democracy, the whole people enjoys that freedom.

It is true that a democratic regime runs the risk that the people will make mistakes. But the risk of mistake exists in all regimes in the real world, and the worst blunders of this century have been made by leaders in nondemocratic regimes. Moreover, the opportunity to make mistakes is an opportunity to learn. Just as we reject paternalism in individual decisions because it prevents the development of our moral capacities, so too we should reject guardianship in public affairs because it will stunt the development of the moral capacities of an entire people. At its best, only the democratic vision can offer the hope, which guardianship can never do, that by engaging in governing themselves, all people, and not merely a few, may learn to act as morally responsible human beings.

# 4

# Is Political Equality Justified?

THE PREVIOUS CHAPTERS lead to three conclusions that taken together create a problem with no evident solution:

1. Existing democratic processes are highly unsatisfactory for dealing with unusually complex issues like nuclear weapons.
2. Those who now make decisions on complex issues do not possess the special knowledge and virtue required for true guardians.
3. True guardians or philosopher-kings, to whom the decisions on all major issues could safely be entrusted, are not at all likely to make such decisions in the future because rulers are not likely to be true philosophers, and true philosophers are not likely to be rulers.

Finding a solution to the problem posed by these conclusions is extraordinarily difficult because of two seemingly irreconcilable facts. The first fact is that in order to deal with nuclear weapons and other complex matters of public policy, some delegation of authority to leaders is unavoidable. The second is that moral and technical judgments are highly interdependent. But because of this interdependence, it is impossible for us simply to delegate authority to leaders to make technical judgments about the most efficient means to ends we approve of, much less establish in advance.

53

In making technical judgments our leaders necessarily make moral judgments that need not be consistent with, and might indeed violate, the moral judgments we would make if we were adequately informed. Nor are these moral judgments of trivial importance: on the contrary, they may decisively determine a choice among the alternatives, as in choosing whether or not to target population centers. The upshot is, then, that delegated authority becomes alienated power.

If the interdependence of instrumental and moral judgments, however, undermines the legitimacy of *de facto* guardians, because they do not possess the superior moral competence required for true guardianship, it also undermines the legitimacy of the democratic process. For if ordinary people lack adequate instrumental competence, and if moral judgments depend on instrumental judgments, then it would appear to follow that they also lack the moral competence to rule. But if they lack the *moral* competence to rule, then they are not qualified to rule. The Strong Principle of Equality, as described in the first chapter, falls, and with it the justification for the democratic process.

What then are we to do? To despair is tempting, but cowardly. I do not think there is an easy answer, and perhaps not even an altogether satisfactory one. To help the search for possible solutions, however, we need to probe more deeply into the problem of moral competence.

## SHOULD PEOPLE BE REGARDED
## AS POLITICAL EQUALS?

It is one thing to reject the case for guardianship. It is quite another to accept the case for the democratic process, particularly when it is meant to be applied to highly complex issues like nuclear weapons. Why should we accept the Strong Principle of Equality?

Given the undeniable fact that people are in so many obvious respects unequal, the claim that they are entitled to be treated as political equals in governing the state is on the face of it preposterous. Innumerable critics have managed to show the folly of democratic ideas, to their own satisfaction, by contrasting with palpable reality the astounding claim of the Declaration of Independence to the self-evident truth of the proposition that all men are created equal. By doing so, however, they have done no more than display their own misunderstanding. For of course the author of those phrases, Thomas Jefferson, knew full well, as was understood long before the Declaration — by John Locke, for example[1] — that the assertion is not to be taken as empirical or factual in the ordinary sense but as a moral-philosophical view about a fundamental, indeed inalienable, entitlement.

Despite the confident words proclaimed in the Declaration, however, the justification for the claim is very far from self evident. The advocates of guardianship deny it: perhaps in few other matters, they will say, are people so obviously unequal as in their competence to rule. So we need to explore the grounds on which one might reasonably rest so seemingly outrageous a claim.

The argument for the Strong Principle of Equality examined here is neither unique nor universal among those who have defended the idea of political equality. Moreover, it exposes a flank to attack by critics of democracy that some advocates, who might prefer to keep it concealed, have sometimes, I think, hidden under a camouflage of rhetoric. But since the camouflage has rarely prevented critics from discovering it, we need to see the argument in plain view.

### The Idea of Equal Intrinsic Worth

Two principles, taken together, provide a sturdy foundation for the Strong Principle of Equality. The first, described in Chapter 2 as a principle on which advocates of democracy and guardianship alike might agree, is the idea of equal intrinsic worth: that no person is intrinsically superior to another, and the good or interests of each human being are entitled to equal consideration. Historically, this principle gained much of its strength, particularly in Europe and the English speaking countries, from the common doctrine of Judaism and Christianity (shared also by Islam) that we are equally God's children. Indeed it was exactly on this belief that Locke grounded his assertion about the natural equality of all persons in a state of nature.[2] When moral reasoning is intended to stand independent of its religious origins, it nevertheless usually maintains that essential premise, as in Jeremy Bentham's well-known axiom, "everybody to count for one, nobody for more than one,"[3] which is an assumption of all utilitarian moral reasoning. What Bentham meant, and what all utilitarians take for granted, is that no matter who Jones and Smith may be, and no matter how the ultimate standard of goodness may be described, whether happiness, pleasure, satisfaction, well-being or utility, Jones's happiness (or whatever) must be counted in exactly the same unit as Smith's. We ought not to measure Jones's happiness in shrunken units because he is an illiterate farm laborer, and Smith's in larger units because he is an artist of exquisitely refined tastes. Even when J. S. Mill contended that some pleasures are better than others, he continued to assume the axiom, for to Mill as to Bentham the relative value of an object or activity depended on its contribution to the pleasure or happiness of the recipient, not on the intrinsic and peculiar worth of the recipient.

Utilitarianism is vulnerable in many ways, of course, and it has always been subjected to heavy attack, particularly by those who try to demonstrate a right course of action, duty, obligation, or right, that is not justified solely by its utilitarian consequences. But these philosophers, from Emmanuel Kant to John Rawls, usually also adopt a premise of equal intrinsic worth.[4]

The persistence and generality of the assumption of equal intrinsic worth in systematic moral reasoning could be attributed to the existence of a norm so deeply embedded in all western cultures that we cannot reject it without denying our cultural heritage, and thereby denying who we are. But a ground for adopting it that appeals less to history and culture and more to its reasonableness is the difficulty of denying it. One could deny it without self-contradiction.[5] But to deny it is to assert, in effect, that some people *are* intrinsically of greater worth, that they are to be regarded and treated as *intrinsically* privileged quite independent of any social contribution they may make. To provide satisfactory reasons for attributing superior intrinsic worth to some person or group of persons is a formidable task, at which no one, to my knowledge, has succeeded.[6]

Standing alone, however, the axiom of equal intrinsic worth

is not robust enough to justify the Strong Principle of Equality. It is weak in at least two ways. In the first place, whatever limits it may set on inequalities are vague and highly elastic. While the axiom means that the life of every other person has the same intrinsic worth as my own, it does not mean that we are all entitled to equal shares or equal treatment, whether in votes, civil rights, medical care, or elsewhere. While it would rule out some allocations, it would allow an immense range. For example, if my neighbor has defective kidneys and needs dialysis in order to survive, equal shares or equal treatment would require that both of us, or neither of us, would be entitled to it, which of course would be nonsensical. Equal votes, equal rights, equal shares, and identical treatment are what Douglas Rae has called "lot-regarding equality," while allocating dialysis to a neighbor who needs it but not to me is "person-regarding equality."[7] The idea of equal intrinsic worth is person-regarding, not lot-regarding. But the Strong Principle of Equality is lot-regarding, not person-regarding.

The second weakness is a consequence of the first. As I have already pointed out, the idea of equal intrinsic worth does not by any means exclude guardianship. For if one believes that a few people not only understand much better than the rest what is in the common good of all, but will also seek to bring it about, then it would be perfectly consistent with the idea of equal intrinsic worth to say that these persons of superior knowledge and virtue should rule over all the others. Even more: if the good of each person is entitled to equal consideration, and if a superior group of guardians could best insure equal consideration, then it follows that guardianship would be desirable.

### The Presumption of Personal Autonomy

If the idea of equal intrinsic worth is, by itself, too weak to support the Strong Principle of Equality, a stout foundation can be constructed by joining it with a second assumption that has been a cornerstone of democratic beliefs, as it has been of liberal thought.[8] This is the assumption that among adults no one else is more likely than oneself, in general, to be a better judge of one's own good or interest, or to act to bring it about. Consequently, among adults everyone should have the right to judge whether a policy or action is, or is not, in one's best interest. Therefore in individual decisions the person for whose benefit a choice is intended should have the last say as to what the choice should be. And the procedures for making collective decisions should also respect that individual's last say. As a result, no adult should ever be required to demonstrate that one is sufficiently competent to protect one's own interests. Instead, the burden of proof must always lie with a claim to an exception, and no exception is admissible in the absence of a very compelling showing. This is *the presumption of personal autonomy.*

Unlike the principle of equal intrinsic worth, which is about as unalloyed a moral judgment as one is likely to encounter, the presumption of personal autonomy is best described as a rule of prudence. A prudential rule is a mix of moral and empirical judgments and thus displays the inherent messiness of a contingent statement that is not derived rigorously from axioms or empirical laws. It draws instead upon a flawed and imprecise understanding of human experience. It does not lay down an absolutely inviolable right or duty, or purport to say what definitely will happen, or estimate precisely what is most likely to happen. It admits of exceptions. But it does tell us where the burden of proof must lie when a claim is made for an exception: that is, for replacing personal autonomy by a paternalistic authority.

In the past, comprehensive paternalism was the general rule for slaves. And until quite recently half of all adults were legally subject to paternalism on grounds widely thought, and not merely by the other half, to be almost self-evident: that women were not competent to make decisions for themselves. Today, however, children are the only general exception to the presumption of personal autonomy. For children, parents are the normal authorities, though in special cases paternalistic authority over a child may be awarded to other adults. For adults, on the other hand, paternalistic authority with respect to individual decisions is thought to be justified only in a small percentage of exceptional cases, persons so severely handicapped because of birth defects, brain damage, acute psychosis, senility, and so on, that they are judged incapable of making the elementary decisions required for their own survival or minimal well-being. Even in these cases, the burden of proof is always legally placed on those who propose to replace personal autonomy by paternalism.

In the case of collective decisions, the ideal standards for the democratic process imply that each citizen has a fundamental, indeed inalienable, right to express his or her own views as to the matters that ought to go on the agenda for collective choice and what the choices among the alternatives on the agenda should be. And members of a losing minority, though required to obey laws passed by a winning majority, are not required to say, much less to believe, that the law is, after all, in their interest (*pace* Rousseau in *The Social Contract*).

All of this is familiar, and so too is the failure in democratic countries always to adhere to democratic procedures. Nonetheless, the presumption of personal autonomy is pretty widely accepted in democratic countries. Yet it is surely not obvious that with highly complex matters like nuclear weapons such a presumption is justified. Given the interdependence between instrumental and moral judgments in these matters, would it not be reasonable to conclude that the burden of proof requirement *is* sufficiently satisfied? Do highly complex questions constitute a reasonable exception to the presumption of personal autonomy? To answer this question, we need to examine various grounds on which the principle is justified.

## Experience

However much we may occasionally doubt individual competence, human experience provides scant support — much less a strong case — for replacing individual autonomy with paternalism among adults. To do so we would have to believe not only that some substantial proportion of adults are quite unable to understand, or are not sufficiently motivated to seek, their most fundamental interests, *but also that a class of paternalistic authorities could be counted on to do so in their behalf.* A moment ago I mentioned the two historic cases that provide the bulk of human experience with comprehensive paternalism — slavery and the legal subjection of women. Do we have the slightest reason for believing that slaves and women would not have protected their own interests at least as well as their masters — and in all likelihood far better?

## Freedom

Added to this powerful negative argument is a powerful positive reason that is all but self-evident: the value of individual freedom. For it is obvious that — as with slavery and the subjection of women — the subjects of paternalistic authority are denied their freedom. And even a more narrowly limited paternalism would deny subjects their freedom over some matters on which others would be free to choose.

## Moral Responsibility and Growth

Because one cannot be responsible for actions over which one has no control, paternalism prevents the exercise of moral responsibility. And by maintaining its subjects in a condition of perpetual childhood, it inhibits the development of a sense of responsibility.

## Incentive

In general, no one has as strong and steady an incentive to seek what is in one's interest as oneself. People may be mistaken as to what *is* in their interest, but they do not often act against what they *believe* to be their interest. To be sure, people may sometimes act in the interests of others, and against their own, but if they do it is mainly when they are closely bonded to the others by ties of love. It would be folly to count on altruism as a steady state in human action. To approve of the golden rule or the categorical imperative is one thing: it is quite another to count on human beings to follow them steadily. We may readily accept the possibility of altruism without making anyone's fate depend on it.

Thus arguments from experience, human incentives, and the values of freedom, moral responsibility, and moral growth all lend support to the presumption of personal autonomy. But the question of *knowledge* is more troublesome.

## Knowledge

If we believe that the adult self is, generally speaking, as capable of apprehending its own interests as any other can do, then the reasons just given would seem to be enough to justify the presumption of personal autonomy, at least for individual decisions. Notice that we do not need to insist that the self is *more* capable than the others: it is enough that, in general, no others are more capable.

None of these justifications for the presumption of personal autonomy would count for much, however, if we believed that many adults are *not* capable, in general, of apprehending their own interests as well as certain others could do. The example of children shows why this is so. The incentives of children to pursue their own interests may be strong, but we nonetheless subject them to parental authority because we believe their understanding is often in error. Believing that children cannot be wholly entrusted with their own freedom, we limit their freedom to make decisions autonomously. And believing that they are not yet capable of assuming full responsibility for their actions, we limit their legal responsibility.

What grounds do we have, then, for believing that in general adults *are* competent to understand their interests? And even if they adequately understand their *own* interests, is it not altogether possible that they may often misunderstand the collective interest or general good of their community, country, or larger collectivity?

Evidently the presumption of personal autonomy presupposes the truth of at least two prior assumptions: (1) In apprehending the good or interest of the self, every other is less advantaged; let us call this *the disadvantaged position of the other*; (2) the collective interest, the common good, the good of all, the good of the community can never be anything other than some combination of individual goods or interests, of what is good for, or in the interests of, the individuals who comprise the collectivity. In order to apprehend the common good of a collectivity, then, we need only to know what is in the good or interest of the persons who comprise the collectivity. We might refer to this as *the person-centered ground for collective interests*.

Once again, however, neither of these assumptions is self-evidently true.

## THE DISADVANTAGED POSITION OF THE OTHER

Is it true that, in general, others are at a disadvantage in apprehending the interests of the self? To ask this question is an invitation to confront one of the most difficult and contentious intellectual problems of our times: Can moral judgments be intellectually justified, and if so how? Few moral philosophers, and probably not many thoughtful and educated people, now believe that absolute, objectively valid and verifiable moral judgments are possible. The few who do have so far not succeeded in demonstrating satisfactorily the absolute and objective status of the moral judgments they assert. At the other extreme, many people appear to believe that moral judgments are wholly subjective and lack all possibility of interpersonal validity. Solutions to this problem have proved elusive and I cannot hope to deal with it here.[9]

However, to justify a claim that some other possesses better knowledge than the self of the self's own good or interests would require one to explain what this knowledge consists of, and to show why it is superior to the knowledge possessed by the self. Relevant knowledge could include knowledge about preferences, wants, needs, or ideal values. Now when we arrange preferences, wants, needs, and ideal values along a hypothetical axis, a significant shift occurs in the kind of knowledge needed. Along most of the axis, the self is uniquely privileged because only the self has direct access to its own awareness. The more that knowledge of self's own interests requires direct access to the self's awareness, the more advantageous is the position of the self. Thus to the extent that the self's own interests are thought to be accurately reflected in the self's own *preferences*, the more valid is the claim of the self to adequate, and even superior, knowledge. Likewise, though expressed preferences might reflect a mistaken view of *wants*, the access of the self to its own awareness again provides a certain advantage. Even if it were the case that the *needs* of human beings form a hierarchy, as some psychologists have maintained, the most that could be reasonably argued is that some needs, say for food, have to be met above a threshold before others take on equal urgency. Yet as a general matter the self is surely in a better position than an other to know the relative order of urgency among its various needs. Indeed, the psychological theory that posits the existence of a hierarchy of needs in human beings makes sense only on the assumption that the relative priorities work their way into the self's awareness, when they can be reported to others. Thus whether based on self's preferences, wants, or needs, the knowledge of the self is likely to be superior to that of any other, and certainly no worse.

Up to now I have deliberately used the terms "interest" and "good" as if they were synonymous. If, however, the *good* of a person consists of something not fully indicated by preferences, wants, or even needs, than the unique access of the self to its own awareness would be less of an advantage. Yet as has already been suggested, it has become notoriously difficult — and some would say impossible — to arrive at objective knowledge about good in this sense. At the very least, several of the most convincing indicators of objectivity are absent: the existence of procedures that experts on the subject agree are appropriate for judging the validity of assertions; among those who use the appropriate procedures, convergence toward agreement on the truth of certain ideas and statements; and a significant body of such truths that are neither trivial nor vacuous but definitely limit the domain of possible choice — about acceptable nuclear strategies, for example. We are therefore entitled, indeed obliged, to look with the greatest suspicion on any claim that an other possesses objective knowledge of the good of the self that is definitely superior to the knowledge possessed by the self.

An additional reason for doubting the validity of another's claim arises if one is confronted, as at times one almost certainly will be, by conflicts between several values, such as seeking one's own happiness or self-development, doing justice to one's family, or doing justice to others. Even if these value conflicts arise within a single, coherent system of values, like utilitarianism, they require judgments about trade offs that depend in turn on detailed knowledge of the particularities of the concrete case. Once again, the self is privileged in its access to the particularities, even the uniqueness, of the self. But value conflicts may also arise because different *systems* of value can and often do specify different courses of action; and no higher order system for adjudicating these conflicts seems to exist.[10] Thus the claim of an other to superior knowledge of what is good for oneself may reflect nothing more than a particular value system, and not at all what would be best in the perspective of the self's own system of values.

### The Dilemma

These reasons seem to me to provide strong grounds for adopting the assumption of personal autonomy as a prudential rule. If the other assumption mentioned earlier is also valid — that the collective interest or common good is no more than a combination of individual interests or goods — then we also have good reasons for believing in the Strong Principle of Equality and thus in the democratic process.

Yet there are at least two reasons for doubting that we are really home safe. First, we have by no means escaped the dilemma suggested at the beginning of this chapter: Whereas instrumental elites lack the special moral competence that might entitle them to make decisions on complex matters of public policy, ordinary people often lack the instrumental knowledge to judge which policies would be in their best interests. On complex issues the interdependence of moral and instrumental judgments seems to leave us with a dilemma from which there is no escape: on complex matters, neither instrumental elites nor ordinary citizens are politically competent to rule.

Could we find a way out if we were to confront the dilemma squarely and search for new political institutions that would improve the political competence of both instrumental elites and citizens? This is the task undertaken in the final chapter.

There is however a second difficulty. Can we really conclude that the common good or general interest is no more than a combination of the interests or goods of the persons who compose the collectivity?

## THE PERSON-CENTERED GROUND
## FOR COLLECTIVE DECISIONS

One might reasonably accept personal autonomy as the general rule for *individual* decisions and yet reject the idea that adults are about equally competent to make *collective* decisions. To know what is best for oneself is not the same as knowing what is best for a collectivity. Perhaps I might know what policy would be best for me even on a quite complex matter. But does it follow that I also know what is best for my country?

The assumption described earlier is person centered: the general good is not something different from the interests or the good of the persons who compose the collectivity. The general good of a community or a nation can then always be decomposed into what is good for the persons in the community or the nation. On this view we are never allowed to smuggle into the general good anything more than the goods of persons. But some people would contend that the general good is something more than, and different from, the good of persons. In this holistic or organic perspective, the general good of at least some collectivities is more than the aggregate good of the persons who constitute the collectivity. The general good, then, cannot always be disaggregated into individual interests or goods. The good of the nation, for example, might be independent of what is good individually for all the persons who make up the nation, past, present, or future.

It might be argued that the organic view is superior to the person-centered view in two ways: because it allows for the value of membership in a community, and because it recognizes that a system, particularly a living system, cannot always be reduced to the sum of its parts. But both criticisms reflect a misunderstanding of the person-centered perspective.

### Community Membership and Collective Interests

Models and theories of society and behavior that emphasize egoism and individualism, and minimize the importance of community ties or collective interests, are no doubt person-centered. However, a person-centered view does not imply egoism or individualism either as fact or value. Surely it is true that membership in a community is a good for almost everyone, if not indeed for everyone. But if so, then this good or interest must be included among the goods or interests of everyone, or nearly everyone. A person's interests may be, and usually are, broader than merely one's *private* or *self-regarding* interests. If the expression "personal interests" is meant to include all of one's interests as a person, then "personal interests" include membership in a community, or nowadays in many communities and collectivities. But the value of community memberships accrues to the persons who compose a community and not to some transcendent organic entity that incurs harm or benefits *independent of the people in it.*

## Communities as Systems, Not Aggregates

It is true also that the properties of a system cannot always be reduced to the properties of the units in a system, since systems consist not only of parts but also of relationships among the parts. Because a community is not simply an aggregate of individual persons but consists also of the relations among them and among the various subsystems, it follows that the characteristics of a community are not reducible to individual characteristics.[11] That a collectivity may have properties that are not reducible to properties of individual persons is not, however, the issue. If we believe that some property of a human system — justice, let us say, or political equality — is valuable, does the value of that quality arise because it benefits the system quite apart from any value it may have for the people in the system, or instead because it benefits the people who compose the system? What one might mean by the first is obscure. If the second is true, however, then a person-centered view will enable us to appreciate the values that might be attributed to certain communities, such as fellowship or justice. Consequently we have no need for an organic perspective, which can add nothing but befuddlement.

## CONCLUSION

To repeat: A powerful justification for the Strong Principle of Equality can be made if two assumptions are accepted as valid: (1) the presumption of personal autonomy, and (2) the person-centered ground for collective decisions. If the Strong Principle of Equality is accepted, then only a little intervening argument (which I shall not introduce here) also justifies political equality and the democratic process.

Yet the presumption of personal autonomy in turn rests on assumptions, some of which may be of dubious validity when citizens attempt to deal with highly complex questions by means of the democratic process — or, at any rate, by means of the conventional political institutions that are now employed as means to the democratic process. At the same time, however, the historical alternative to the democratic process, a system of guardianship, is also rendered unsatisfactory by inescapable limitations on the knowledge and virtue of the putative guardians.

The more deeply we have probed, the more elusive a solution to this dilemma seems to have become. Nonetheless, difficult as it may be to find a wholly satisfactory solution, we have an obligation to see whether we might deal better with complex questions than we do at present.

# 5

# Vision of a Possible Future

I F WE BELIEVE that human beings are of equal intrinsic worth
(though not, by virtue of that quality, necessarily also of equal
competence) then we should aspire to a political system that is consistent with this assumption. In principle, both democracy and
guardianship could be so. Democracy could make it possible for
people to protect their own interests, or good, by means of the
democratic process. Guardianship could make it possible for an
elite of knowledge and virtue to know and protect the interests
of all. In practice, however, because of defects in both the knowledge and virtue of the guardians, we have strong and sufficient
grounds for doubting that they would in fact serve the interests
of all, or the public good. But likewise we have good reasons for
thinking that some complex issues of great importance cannot be
decided wisely without instrumental knowledge that is, at present, well beyond the reach of most citizens. Moreover, citizens may
not possess an understanding of their own goals, and how these
bear on the issues, that is well developed enough to offer them
much guidance in deciding among alternative policies.

## LIMITED GUARDIANSHIP?

The classical case for guardianship argues for a regime in which
the guardians are sovereign and rule over *all* public matters, a re-

gime justified by the assumption that a minority exists, or could be created, that would be definitely more qualified to rule than the rest. Perhaps a weaker assumption might lead to a stronger case. Suppose we accept the more reasonable claim that on questions of exceptional complexity, like nuclear weapons, a small minority of highly qualified people could be found, or could be created by education and selection, who would pretty clearly possess superior judgment on these complex matters. Suppose that instead of complete sovereignty, these people — call them quasi-guardians — were to have jurisdiction only over a limited and specific sphere of policies, like nuclear weapons.

Without attempting to offer a blueprint for such a solution, let me suggest the U. S. Supreme Court as a rough analogy. It is no great distortion to say that by design and in actual practise the justices are quasi-guardians. By design they are intended to be insulated from the democratic process. Because the justices are appointed by the president and confirmed by the senate, in practise the court's policies are sooner or later brought into conformity with those of an enduring coalition of the president and a senate majority. Sometimes, however, the interval is quite long; in the extreme case, a generation elapsed before a majority of justices upheld the constitutionality of legislation outlawing child labor. If we had a mind to, we could design a constitutional system of quasi-guardianship in which something like the Supreme Court would exercise exclusive jurisdiction over all policies and decisions within, let us say, the field of nuclear weapons. I do not mean a regulatory agency in the familiar American pattern, that is, a body deliberately designed to be subject through legislation to the control of Congress and president. I mean a body like the Supreme Court that would be deliberately designed to be as immune as possible to any external political influence and subject only to its own judgments. The aim would be to appoint to it — perhaps by some process even more insulated from indirect popular influence than appointments to the Supreme Court — the persons best qualified to make decisions about highly complex questions requiring both instrumental and moral judgments: the quasi-guardians.[1]

Would some system of quasi-guardianship be a satisfactory solution? It seems doubtful, for several reasons. To begin with, some practical difficulties would have to be overcome. How would the quasi-guardians be appointed and, if need be, removed? If by elected officials (if, for example, as with justices of the Supreme Court the president had the power to "nominate, and by and with the advice and consent of the Senate . . . appoint" them) it is hard to imagine that the process would not be even more highly politicized than is now the case with judicial appointments. But if not by elected officials, by whom? And who would determine which issues properly fall within their jurisdiction? Furthermore, how would the decisions of different groups of quasi-guardians be coordinated and reconciled? If the quasi-guardians in charge of nuclear weapons decisions decide that a new weapon must be produced and deployed — call it the X-missile — and the quasi-guardians in charge of strategic arms negotiations, let us say, decide that the weapon ought not to be produced because it would diminish the chances for an arms control agreement, who is to decide? Superguardians? But do we not then in effect create a regime of full guardianship, which would be heir to all the objections discussed in the last chapter?

More important, if all highly complex issues were turned over to groups of quasi-guardians what would be left for the democratic process? While quasi-guardianship would drift toward full guardianship, quasi-democracy would drift toward nondemocracy.

In addition, once again we face the fundamental inadequacy of the guardians' knowledge. Despite all the limitations of specialized knowledge, it is surely true that in most areas of policy specialists might be found whose instrumental knowledge is greatly superior to that of most citizens, and even most elected officials. Yet as we have seen in the case of nuclear weapons, instrumental knowledge, however necessary it may be to wise decisions, is not sufficient. For just as with full guardianship, so too the quasi-guardians must inevitably base their judgments about policy on assumptions about ends, moral standards, values. These assumptions are in no wise rendered less crucial by the fact that the quasi-guardians make decisions within a restricted area of policy rather than across the whole domain of public policies. Recall the fearfully difficult moral judgments our *de facto* guardians must make, implicitly or explicitly, in choosing among alternative policies for nuclear weapons. Yet we have no grounds for thinking that specialists possess moral understanding superior to that of others. To the contrary, we have good reasons for believing that the keen edge

of moral understanding may sometimes be blunted by specialization of knowledge, function, and loyalty.

Finally, once again we confront doubts about the superior
virtue of the quasi-guardians: their willingness to act in behalf of
a broader good that might conflict with narrower or more short
run benefits to the quasi-guardians themselves. As we have seen,
even with nuclear weapons, where no policy-maker in his right
mind can count on surviving (and might not even believe that survival in the aftermath of nuclear destruction is particularly desirable), bureaucratic rivalries and loyalties sometimes seem to
outweigh broader considerations.

The upshot is that while quasi-guardianship and full guardianship are similar in their potential virtues, they are too much alike
in their potential vices. Having rejected full guardianship because
of the weakness of its claims, it will not do to accept a more pallid
version that suffers from much the same defects.


## THE PROBLEM RESTATED

A solution that would satisfy democratic criteria would seem to
require at least three things: First, citizens should possess sufficient *competence*, both moral and instrumental, to make adequately enlightened judgments either about policies or about the
terms on which authority to make decisions may safely be delegated. Second, given a satisfactory level of competence, citizens
should be able to exercise sufficient *control* during the process of
decision making to insure that the final decision corresponds with
their informed intentions. Literally interpreted, the second requirement makes the third unnecessary. If, however, we assume that
some delegation is inevitable, and that delegation will inevitably
create some opportunity for an abuse of authority, then we shall
need a third requirement: Those to whom authority is delegated
should be motivated to seek the goals implied by the informed intentions of citizens, or the greater number of them, rather than
merely their own private interests or even their own private con-
ceptions of the public good.

Each of these three requirements is highly demanding. Each
is potentially a vast topic in itself. Whether the first is attainable,
and if so how, has been the central question in this exploration

of the conflict between the idea of democracy and the idea of guardianship. Unless the first is satisfied, the second and third lose much of their point. For these reasons, this final chapter will consider how the first requirement might be met.

Our aim, then, is to develop a body of citizens who are competent to make adequately enlightened judgments either about the public issues themselves, or about the terms on which they may safely delegate to others the authority to make decisions.

By adequately enlightened I do not mean to suggest anything like perfect rationality or complete knowledge, both of which are humanly unattainable. I mean rather that every citizen should be able to answer four kinds of questions:

What kinds of problems do I confront for which government action is necessary or desirable?

For a given problem or a set of problems, what are the relevant alternative solutions that I ought to consider? What are the likely results of each? What is the relative likelihood that the expected consequences will actually come about? How much confidence should I place in the estimates or "guesstimates?"

Considering the answers to these questions, and my own values, what relative value should I assign to each alternative? My values, it should be pointed out, include the value I attach to the good or interests of others, and the community to which I belong. They also include the value I attach to taking risks, or avoiding them.

To whom and on what terms can I safely delegate decisions on matters that I cannot reasonably hope to decide wisely?

These are the standard questions posed in idealized versions of the policymaking process. Although some policymakers might proceed systematically to gain satisfactory answers to questions like these, and perhaps many more might be able to do so if they chose, most citizens would face tremendous obstacles if they tried and few citizens do try.

## SOME UNSATISFACTORY SOLUTIONS

### Participation and Discussion

The usual panacea is to try to increase citizen participation in policymaking. Now it is undeniable that large numbers of citizens do not participate actively in public life except by voting, and even in elections, as everyone knows, the American turnout is low by comparative standards. As a consequence citizen control over governmental decisions is much weaker than it might be. But as I suggested earlier, to solve the problem of *citizen control* would not by itself solve the problem of *citizen competence*. Simply to increase participation means only that more people participate in decisions without understanding what the alternatives are or which alternatives would best achieve their values. It is often asserted that participation itself will increase civic competence. There may be some truth in this view, if what is meant is that by participating, citizens will learn the ropes and gain some confidence in their political skills. Although these are worthwhile objectives, to accomplish them would not solve our problem. It might be said that participation will also tend to enhance understanding of public issues. Again there may be some truth in this conjecture. But mere participation in ways available to most citizens will not provide them with adequate understanding of complex issues. Lying behind the hope for political participation as an educative force there is sometimes, I suspect, a conception of a process of *discussion* in a highly idealized town meeting or Athenian assembly. But discussion with other equally uninformed citizens will not solve the problem we confront.[2]

### Education

A favorite American solution for almost any problem is to prescribe more education. In the broadest meaning of the term, that is of course exactly what is required. But in the more conventional sense, to look to education is unpromising for at least three reasons. First, raising average levels of educational competence would take a very long time. Second, even so, people would have widely varying levels of educational achievement, cognitive skills, and the like. Finally, even if one were to strain credulity and imagine that practically everyone has an advanced degree, citizens would still vary enormously in their specific knowledge. Physicists would still know a great deal more than the rest of us about physics, mathematicians about mathematics, geneticists about genetics, and so on. These variations in knowledge would mean that nuclear physicists, for example, might be highly competent on certain aspects of public issues that intersected with particle physics, but quite possible incompetent on every other aspect.

### Better Decision Makers

A vast amount of attention has been given since Plato's time to the problem of improving the quality and performance of public officials, whether guardians in a Platonic republic or elected officials and civil servants in a democratic republic. But to improve the quality and performance of policy analysts and decision makers does nothing to improve the performance of ordinary citizens. Greater virtue and wisdom among leaders is surely desirable, and may be a necessary ingredient to a satisfactory solution, but it is not sufficient.

### A Policy Science?

In the last several decades Plato's royal science of government has found its modern echo in aspirations for a policy science. But so far, as twenty-five hundred years ago with Plato, aspiration has greatly exceeded accomplishment. Indeed, many writers on policy science turn Plato on his head. Where he insisted that instrumental knowledge was subordinate to philosophy and knowledge of the good, they are more likely to write as if the technical or instrumental aspects were paramount, and give little more than lip service to problems of value.[3]

## SKETCH OF A QUASI-UTOPIAN SOLUTION

A moment ago I suggested four questions that a competent citizen should be able to answer. I now want to draw a sketch of a set of institutions that could, I believe, greatly improve the capacities of citizens to answer these questions. In doing so, I am going to look for solutions much closer to ideal possibilities than we are accustomed to discuss seriously. Some people will see these solutions as utopian. They may be right, though possibly for the wrong reasons. Nothing that I am going to propose is beyond our reach; but much of it lies beyond our vision. The technology assumed here is at hand; it is certain to be shaped to *some* human purposes. But it may not be shaped to good purposes, and quite possibly we may lack the will to shape it to democratic purposes. The aim of my quasi-utopian proposals is to adapt technology to an urgent democratic goal, the fostering of politically competent citizens. In what follows, however, my concern is not so much that the details are right but that a seemingly utopian sketch of human possibilities may stimulate further thought, and even action, so that what is now within our reach may soon become within our grasp.

What I am going to suggest is a set of organizations and processes to accomplish three objectives:

1. To insure that information about the political agenda, appropriate in level and form, and accurately reflecting the best knowledge available, is easily and universally accessible to all citizens;

2. To create easily available and universally accessible opportunities to all citizens to influence the informational agenda, and to participate in a relevant way in political discussions;

3. To provide a highly informed body of public opinion that (except for being highly informed) is representative of the entire citizen body.

## LEARNING

Let me turn to the first objective, which itself consists of three parts.

### Information Easily and Universally Accessible to All Citizens

In 1981, 97 percent of all households in the United States had telephones, 99 percent had radio sets (an almost unbelievable average of 5.5 sets for each household), and 98 percent had television sets, which were viewed on the average some 6.7 hours a day.[4] It is or soon will be possible in this country for any citizen[5] to engage in political discussion with any other citizen and, within the limits that time imposes on any discussion, with groups of citizens, wherever they may be. For example, a town meeting could be convened of a thousand citizens scattered across the length and breadth of the United States. Even more important, every citizen could have easy two-way access to politically relevant information.

Efforts that have already been made to exploit the present technology of telecommunications to facilitate citizen participation in public life tell us something about both limits and possibilities. To those who identify the problem simply as one of participation, telecommunications can provide citizens with unlimited opportunities to express their preferences — that is, to vote. Some writers like R. P. Wolff have proposed nearly instantaneous national plebiscites as a means to participatory democracy.[6] But as I have already argued, merely increasing citizen participation, whether by electronic means or others, does not confront the issue of citizen competence: A plebiscite is no guarantee that citizens understand the issue on which they are voting.[7] In the Qube system used in Columbus, Ohio, and some neighboring towns, paying subscribers to the Warner-Amex cable channel, Qube Columbus, are provided with a push-button console that allows them to indicate answers to questions posed on their television screen. The console allows one of five possible responses, and a central computer can tally responses within ten seconds. But the system does not enable viewers to participate in discussion, the viewers who punch the buttons need not have watched much of the preceding program, the programs are not always informative, the questions posed to viewers are necessarily simplified, and only a fraction of eligible voters participate.[8]

More indicative of potentialities are systems that allow for dialogue. One of these in Reading, Pennsylvania uses no advanced technology at all. Berks Community Television (BCTV) provides weekly programs in which public officials may be asked questions by viewers. For example, on "Inside City Hall" five members of the city council discuss various subjects with a moderator. Viewers may use an open phone line to question the councilmen, or in fact to say anything they wish. According to one report, "To an extraordinary degree, the viewers control the agenda, asking as many follow-up questions as they want, offering their own opinions, or raising new subjects."[9]

A system established five years ago by the State of Alaska provides much greater opportunity for dialogue between citizens and officials. Because of the state's huge size and the inaccessibility of the capital, Juneau, located in the extreme southeastern panhandle, the state has created eighty four centers at which citizens may observe officials in Juneau and engage in discussion with them by means of manned computers. For example, a citizen in the Aleutians can watch a hearing held by a legislative committee in Juneau, and immediately pose a question, raise an objection, or supply a comment. In keeping perhaps with the egalitarian spirit of Alaskan life, it is common practice for the citizen's comments to be taken up at once and discussed. Thus a genuine dialogue can and frequently does occur.[10]

Competence, it was suggested above, requires that information be easily and universally accessible to all citizens. Experiences like those just described are less relevant for what they have achieved than for their hint of possible achievements. While their aim is to enhance citizen participation, ours here is to improve citizen competence. Let me then sketch out a possible future.

A citizen wonders what the main issues are in current politics, or wants to know something about a particular issue, or is uncertain where she stands on a current question. She turns to an interactive public television channel, asks for political information, and receives a menu of options. She chooses "issues" and receives three responses. One is a list of issues ranked from "most important" to "least important" generated by a random sample of 1600 citizens, much as Gallup now presents from time to time. The second is a list of issues prepared by an advisory commission of scholars. I will say something more about these advisory commissions in a moment. The third response is an offer to list the issues that other people who are like her in some important ways feel are important. To receive this third list she checks off the personal characteristics she thinks are most relevant: let us say, gender, race, education, job, income.

If she prefers print to screen, she may ask that the lists be printed out on a printer tied to the interactive channel and located at her home or in the nearest public building. Having examined the lists, she wants to learn something about one of the issues. What she can now receive is relevant information, appropriate to her capacities both in level and in form, that accurately reflects the best knowledge available in the society.

## Information Appropriate in Level and Form

One of the most elementary and universally accepted principles of education is that teaching and learning must be adapted to the capacities of students. The most obvious application of this elementary principle is to place students in grades according to age and achievement. Initially age is the dominant criterion; but with increasing education it tends to yield to achievement, the dominant criterion in all higher education. In doctoral programs, for example, age is virtually irrelevant: a child genius of fourteen and an octogenarian might both receive their doctoral degrees at the same ceremony.

Yet even though politically relevant information is churned out in the United States and other advanced societies in many forms and at many levels, no systematic effort is made to insure that civic teaching and learning are appropriately adapted to the individual capacities of citizens. Whatever adaptation may take place is largely left to the citizen, much as if we were to assign teachers randomly to schools and classrooms and turn students loose to find the subject and the teacher best matched to their particular needs and capacities.

As a result, a great deal of politically relevant information, perhaps most, is simply not appropriate to the cognitive and educational levels of a significant part of an audience. If a presentation meets the needs of the best informed, it is likely to be over the heads of the poorly informed — and vice versa. Moreover the *form* of the presentation may itself be inappropriate. A functional illiterate — and an appalling number of American citizens are functionally illiterate[11] — will need speech or visually comprehensible presentations rather than writing. Such a citizen might be best served by an animated cartoon or the equivalent of "Sesame Street." It is also the case that some of us gain information most easily by reading, others through discussion, others by means of a lecture, and so on. Moreover, for any one of us, the form best suited to our needs and capacities may vary with the subject and the difficulty of the content.

Would it somehow violate the Strong Principle of Equality if we were to assume that citizens are not equally capable of coping with information presented at a given level of difficulty? This principle, as we have seen, is one reason for preferring democracy to guardianship. But as we have also seen, the inordinate complexity of some public matters also calls the principle into question. If the principle were interpreted to say that most people over an arbitrary age of reason such as eighteen are about equally well informed on public matters then it is manifestly absurd. Even if it were interpreted more reasonably to mean that given identical opportunities to participate in public discussions about public matters, and about the same utilization of these opportunities, most adults would be about equally well informed, the assumption would be dubious. But would the principle be violated in any way if we were to say that all citizens should have an equally and easily available alternative to learn about public matters *at a level and in a form appropriate to their capacities*?

Let me offer a few illustrative examples to suggest how the need for information appropriate in both level and form might be met.

Imagine that with the interactive system of telecommunications I described earlier, a citizen indicates that he has a high school education and would like to see and hear a discussion, lasting about an hour, during which the various alternatives are fairly represented. After watching and listening to the discussion, he asks for a print-out of certain facts, observations, or arguments offered during the discussion. When he discovers that some of these are presented in a way too difficult for him to grasp, he asks for them in a more easily understood graphical form. Even the graphics, he discovers, are a bit too difficult, and he requests and receives a simpler and more understandable version.

The opportunity to obtain information in a suitable form is essential. Many people engaged in higher education are inclined to assume that learning necessarily requires the standard means of communicating information — speech, the printed word, or perhaps two-dimensional illustrations. But for some purposes these are very far from satisfactory. A documentary drama like "The Day After" made it possible for more people to learn more about the likely outcome of nuclear war than the millions of words uttered orally or in print over the preceding thirty eight years.

Let me suggest an even less conventional but also perhaps less controversial possibility. Architects often construct a small scale three dimensional model to suggest how the spatial forms they propose might look on a larger scale. Yet as everyone who has ever built a house knows, small three dimensional models by no means provide a satisfactory equivalent to the actual building. The discrepancy between the way in which one experiences a model and the actual construction is particularly evident with very large buildings in a complex setting of other structures and spaces, as in a town, a university campus, or a city. To the despair of city planners, the discrepancy is often spectacularly evident when a whole new complex of forms and spaces is created, as in urban redevelopment. In order to make intelligent decisions in these cases — in urban redevelopment, for example — we would need to do what on the face of it looks to be impossible, to experience the forms and spaces *before* they are built in order to decide whether we are going to like the forms and spaces after they are built.

Yet here too technology brings this seeming impossibility within reach. In the Environmental Simulation Laboratory at the University of California, Berkeley, a computer moves a camera both horizontally and vertically over scale models of proposed structures. Using a device invented for the movie industry, a viewer can simulate a walk along a street or around a building, or by changing the shutter speed one may move along a street or highway at the speed of an automobile. One illuminating result is that when the models constructed by architecture students are simulated in the way just described, the students are sometimes unable to identify their own models. Residents of the Sunset District in San Francisco used the laboratory to see whether a proposed sewer line along the ocean beach would block their view, as they had expected it would. When they discovered that it would not, they dropped their objections. It has been used to see what effect a highway and bridge near Shreveport, Louisiana would have on the landscape. It is said to have been "crucial in developing San Francisco's new downtown plan." Recently, in a simulation of a drive through downtown Los Angeles, it was found that with only a few changes in the positions of one or two buildings, elderly people rapidly became lost.[12]

It would of course be absurd to say that the proper use of this technology would solve all the problems of citizen participation in and control over urban planning and development. The solution does strike me, however, as an extraordinary innovation that could enable citizens to participate much more competently in decisions about the shape of their spatial environment.

### Information Accurately Reflecting the Best Knowledge

As I suggested in the first chapter, for much of our political information today we rely on a partisan, adversarial process that was largely developed in the nineteenth century, though it did of course have antecedents. Although such a process may be necessary, for reasons that I indicated earlier today it is insufficient, particularly for dealing with highly complex issues. The adversarial process presupposes that the truth will out as the adversaries contend for our attention and support. The result is, however, that most of the information presented by the advocates, as we see so clearly during the quadrennial contests for the nomination and election of a president, is highly biased and manipulative. It is true that well-educated people can by persistent search discover knowledge that approximates the best available. But many highly educated people do not do so, while less educated citizens often rely on wholly inadequate information.

Although the technology now or soon at hand might make political information appropriate in level and form easily available to every citizen, it is obvious that technology by itself is no guarantee of the quality of the information that is made available. Technology is often neutral; but the purposes to which it is put are not neutral. We can be reasonably sure that new techniques of communication will be used somehow, by some people, for some purposes, for the benefit of some interests. But we have little ground for assuming that they will be used for benign purposes, unless we deliberately shape the institutions that determine their use.

What should such institutions be? A hint of possibilities is suggested by the National Academy of Sciences. The National Academy was incorporated by an act of Congress signed by Abraham Lincoln in 1863. A brief act of three paragraphs specified the original members by name, and granted the organization virtually full autonomy, including the selection of members. It also declared, however, that "the Academy shall, whenever called upon by any department of the Government, investigate, examine, experiment, and report upon any subject of science or art. . . ."

Although the expenses for such investigations were to be paid by the government, the act explicitly stated that "the Academy shall receive no compensation whatever for any services to the Government of the United States."[13]

Today the academy has about 1400 members and 200 foreign associates. Through an elaborate process of nominations and elections existing members choose new members annually. Election to the academy is regarded among American scientists as one of the highest honors that can be bestowed by scientists on scientists. Because of its special role in providing analyses of many kinds, the academy, jointly with its corresponding organizations, the National Academy of Engineering and the Institute of Medicine, also exercises control over the National Research Council. The NRC contains four "assemblies" and four "commissions." For example, the Assembly of Behavioral and Social Sciences was organized in 1973 not only to advance the disciplines under that general rubric but also "to bring to bear the knowledge, analytical tools, and methods of the behavioral and social sciences upon the nation's major problems in efforts to understand them better and to assist in their alleviation."[14] Under the auspices of the academy and the National Research Council an extraordinary number of committees, boards, and panels, drawing on the unpaid participation of the country's best professional intellect, devote their attention to issues of public policy, from aging or alcoholism to hazardous wastes, safe drinking water, women, and youth.[15] Their reports are generally of high quality, about as objective as one could reasonably expect, and moderately influential.

Although the academy is unique in its obligation to respond to government requests for investigation, it is by no means unique in several other crucial respects. The American Philosophical Society — not to be confused with the American Philosophical Associa-

tion, the professional organization for academic philosophers —
was founded in Philadelphia "for Promoting Useful Knowledge"
in 1769.[16] Like the National Academy of Sciences, election to the
society is intended to confer an honor on people who have distinguished themselves in the sciences, humanities, creative arts, or
public affairs, and is if anything even more fully autonomous than
the academy. A third organization of this kind is the American
Academy of Arts and Sciences in Boston. A different type of organization, but one relevant to our concerns here, is the professional association of scholars in a discipline. I have already mentioned the professional association for academic philosophers, but
there are many others, in economics, political science, psychology,
physics, chemistry, and so on, almost without number. Although
limits on membership in these professional associations tend to be
nominal and many are open to almost anyone willing to pay the
membership fee, they are, like the honorary societies, more or less
completely autonomous. Finally, it is worth mentioning certain
organizations whose boards are selected with the concurrence of
the professional scholarly associations: the American Council of
Learned Societies, for example, and the Social Science Research
Council.

All these organizations share certain characteristics: They are
composed pirmarily of scholars and are responsive to the needs
and values of scholars, they are internally pluralistic and usually
reflect the major intellectual currents and controversies of the field,
and they are probably about as independent of external controls
as any organizations in our society, including churches and uni-
versities. Indeed, an overt attempt to control or manipulate them
from outside — by the government, economic organizations, political parties, or other interest organizations — would trigger off enormous opposition. It seems fair to say that they could be brought
to heel by nothing short of an authoritarian regime. In that event,
the problem of civic learning we are concerned with here would
no longer be relevant.

Because of their independence and intellectual resources, these
associations could contribute in an important way to civic learning. Imagine that the societies were to appoint members to the
advisory commissions of scholars mentioned earlier. One of these
advisory commissions could describe the major issues that, in its

view, citizens need to confront. This description of issues, you may recall, is only one of three that our citizen would receive through her telecommunication network. With respect to each of these issues, another advisory commission would describe the relevant alternatives, estimate the likely consequences of each, assess the reliability of these estimates, call attention to the relevant values, and monitor the preparation and presentation of the informational programs.[17] Thus it insures among other things that the more elementary levels and forms of presentation are an acceptably accurate reflection of the knowledge available, within the limits set, of course, by the need for simplification.[18]

## INFLUENCING THE AGENDA

How might we attain the second objective: to insure easily available and universally accessible opportunities for all citizens to influence the informational agenda, and to participate in a relevant way in political discussions?

Although citizens would find it far easier to acquire information and improve their political understanding with the aid of the organizations and processes just described, they would not necessarily confront any greater opportunities to participate in political life more actively. However, it would be comparatively easy to make it possible for citizens to participate more directly in helping to influence the agenda of the advisory commissions system. If the process were interactive, citizens could indicate matters that in their view were omitted or inadequately handled. Rules could be established to insure that any matters on which a sufficient number of citizens indicated a common concern would be dealt with by an advisory commission. Although practical problems would inevitably arise, it is hard to believe that these could not be overcome.

As the project in the State of Alaska mentioned a moment ago suggests, citizens could also influence the agenda of political decision making even more directly: they could participate directly in hearings by means of telecommunications. The Alaskan system looks particularly promising whenever the number of citizens involved is small and their assembling together is difficult, either because they are widely dispersed over a huge area as in the extreme case of Alaska, or because they are elderly and perhaps infirm, as with elderly citizens in Reading, Pennsylvania, or for other reasons.

However, if the number of citizens grows large and decentralization of the process to smaller groups is for some reason undesirable, then a solution is less straightforward, since citizen inquiries and proposals would have to be combined or aggregated in some fashion. Yet a process of aggregating views — totalling the numbers on one side or another of a question — would impede the give and take characteristic of the process in Alaska, where any citizen stands a reasonable chance of having her question put almost immediately to a legislative committee member. Although the effects of increasing numbers cannot be wholly eradicated, ways of coping suggest themselves. For example, questions raised by citizens who observe a congressional hearing on Wednesday might be aggregated and placed on the agenda for Thursday. Priority on the agenda might also be assigned according to the relative number of persons who concur on a question or proposal.

## REPRESENTING PUBLIC OPINION

Finally, how can we possibly achieve the third objective, which on the face of it looks self-contradictory: to provide a highly informed body of public opinion that *except for being highly informed* is *representative* of the entire citizen body?

Certainly the solutions described thus far could substantially raise the average level of civic understanding of complex issues, increase the size and representativeness of attentive elites, improve the quality of public discussion and debate, and help to make political elites, both elective and bureaucratic, responsive to a more informed body of citizens. Yet even if everything I have suggested were in place and working satisfactorily, the problem that has emerged in these essays as a central and formidable obstacle to the democratic process — the interdependence of moral and technical judgments — would not necessarily be satisfactorily solved. The organizations and processes sketched out here would hardly provide for a systematic exploration, in depth, of the interdependent moral and technical questions involved in complex issues.

Because of the limitations of elections mentioned in the first chapter, and despite the numerous ways in which public opinion helps to influence the agenda of political decisions as well as the decisions themselves, it is often crucial to the democratic process for both citizens and officials to know what alternative would be favored by, or at least acceptable to, a majority of citizens. Advocates of plebiscitary democracy would of course make government policy highly dependent on referenda. Yet even if public opinion were to reflect considerably greater competence on public matters than is now the case, referenda and other techniques of direct democracy would tend to suffer, like opinion surveys, from many of the defects we are trying to remedy. One view of participatory democracy assumes by implication that *all* citizens, or most of them at any rate, would somehow come to possess a high degree of political competence on *all* major issues — something approximating the competence, let us say, of a well informed member of Congress. But this looks to be flatly impossible. Arguably it is not even a particularly worthy ideal. After all, political life is not the whole of life, and all of us ought not to be obliged to devote all of our daily lives to becoming extraordinarily well-informed and active citizens.

A more attainable and perhaps even more desirable alternative might be adopted. Imagine that a representative group of citizens were to acquire a high degree of political competence and were to "stand for," and in this sense of the term to "represent," the rest. But in order to "stand for" the citizen body as a whole, so far as humanly possible they ought not to develop additional interests stemming from the very role of representation itself, such as a primary interest in re-election. To avoid this possibility, and to insure that their interests were essentially no other than the interests they possess as ordinary citizens, citizens would need to be chosen randomly, and for a limited period. Election by lot is an ancient democratic idea that preceded elected representation by several thousand years. So to insure that our representative bodies of citizens were truly representative, its members would be chosen by a random process, rather like respondents are chosen in scientifically designed opinion surveys.

We might call such a body a *minipopulus*. As to the size of a minipopulus, suppose we say about a thousand: a compromise between the lower limits set by the risk of excessive sampling error and upper limits set by opportunities to participate in discussion. In my experience, a thousand is large for a town meeting, but manageable. One minipopulus might decide on the agenda of issues, while several others might each concern itself with one of the major issues. A minipopulus could exist at any level of government: national, state or local. Citizens selected for membership in a minipopulus would be paid. They would serve for a year — and no more than once in a lifetime.

Members of a minipopulus would not need to assemble in one place, for they could easily meet instead by means of telecommunications. Indeed, it would be advantageous for them to remain in their own communities, with their own friends and acquaintances. They could meet for a year, let us say, during which they would be expected to work through a single important issue. Each minipopulus could be attended — again by telecommunications — by an advisory committee of scholars chosen along the lines suggested earlier, and by an administrative staff monitored by the advisory committee. A minipopulus could hold hearings, commission research, and engage in debate and discussion.

By the end of its year, a minipopulus could indicate the preference ordering of its members among the most relevant alternatives in the policy area assigned to it. Its "decision" however, would have no binding effect — on the relevant legislature or executive, for example. For a minipopulus would not be a law making or rule making body. Rather it would "stand for" the public: it would represent what the public would itself prefer if members of the public were as well informed as the members of the minipopulation had become. A minipopulus would reflect public opinion at a higher level of competence.

A vital task of a minipopulus would be to assess *risks, uncertainties, and trade offs*. As we saw in Chapter 3, on these crucial presuppositions of policy decisions, specialists can make no special claim to expertise. On many important issues, to arrive at judgments requires assumptions about the world and its tendencies, the relative worth of lives, present and future, under alternative circumstances and conditions that may be highly uncertain and radically different from one another, and how much risk and uncertainty it is prudent to accept in the hope of achieving the best possible outcome. Decisions about nuclear weapons strategies are of course jampacked with such crucial presuppositions. So too are many other complex issues. Who could justifiably claim to possess a more reasonable judgment on these matters than a minipopulus that had grappled with the issue for a year?

The relevant decision makers, whether congress and president, a state governor and legislature, or mayor and council, could and at times probably would disagree with the majority views expressed by the minipopulus, particularly if no overwhelming consensus had emerged. In disagreeing, however, decision makers would need to explain their reasons for doing so, and in this way their disagreement would itself contribute still further to the continuing process of civic teaching and learning.

## CONCLUSION

Whether the solutions sketched out here are the best that could be suggested, I cannot say. I assume that further discussion, inquiry, and experience might well lead to better solutions. Nor would I expect any proposals that might be suggested along these lines to be adopted in the near future on a large scale in this country or in any other. For not only will proposals like these appear to most people as too utopian to be seriously considered, but prudence argues that small scale experiments should precede large scale adoption.

The intention of this book is to identify and clarify a problem of considerable urgency, the problem of citizen competence, to sketch a possible solution, to invite further inquiry, and if possible, to stimulate experiments from which firmer conclusions might be drawn.

The argument of this book has been animated by the hope that the ancient vision, now twenty-five centuries old, of a people governing itself through the democratic process, and possessing all the resources and institutions necessary in order to govern itself wisely, can be adapted yet once again, as it has been in the past, to a world drastically different from the world in which that vision was first put into practice. For I believe that through adaptation, in the twenty-first century, among no insignificant number of people, democracy will be seen, and will continue to be practiced, as the best attainable regime—when all is weighed and considered, one definitely superior to its ancient, enduring, and formidable rival, the ideal of guardianship.

# Appendixes

## APPENDIX 1  PUBLIC OPINION AND NUCLEAR WEAPONS

During most of the period since 1945 few systematic surveys were made of public opinion about issues of nuclear weapons strategy and control. Although this can hardly be taken as conclusive evidence that little public opinion on these issues existed, it does strongly suggest that possibility, since Gallup and other survey organizations are attentive to issues of salience in American politics. In response to a standard Gallup question — What do you think is the most important problem facing the nation? — from 1973 to 1981 respondents showed no sign of concern about nuclear weapons or war.[1] In March 1982, 5 percent gave answers that could be classifed as "fear of war." This figure increased through 1983 and peaked in November 1983 — shortly following "The Day After," which was viewed by roughly half of all U.S. adults — at 26 percent, second only to unemployment (31 percent).[2] In the Gallup Feburary 10–13, 1984 poll the fear of war was down to 11 percent.[3]

Surveys of opinions about the Salt II agreement during 1979 produced substantial differences in support, depending on the wording of the question (*Public Opinion*, March/May 1979, p. 27). Variations of this kind usually signify that attitudes are labile and weakly structured, often a function of low information and understanding of the issues. The low level of information and understanding of nuclear policy questions is also indicated by the small proportion of the public who correctly identified the U.S. and USSR as parties to Salt II. The proportion rose in November 1979 to only 38 percent, up from 23 percent in January 1977. By comparison, those with no opinion (44 percent) or completely incorrect identification (4 percent) remained close to a majority in November 1979, a small decline from January 1977, when the figures were 53 percent with no opinion and 6 percent with incorrect identifications (CBS/*New York Times*, January 1979 and June 1979). Senate hearings on Salt II beginning in July evidently made the agreement considerably more salient. In March 1979, 58 percent said they had heard or read about Salt II, while in July the figure was 82 percent and in September 81 percent.[4]

A marked increase in the frequency of surveys on nuclear issues began with the emergence of the freeze movement around 1980. For the first time since 1945, nuclear weapons control became a salient political issue. In May 1982, in response to the question, "Have you been paying much attention to the issue of a nuclear freeze or not?," 53 percent said yes, 45 percent no, and 2 percent had no opinion. However, 32 percent mistakenly identified President Reagan as favoring a nuclear freeze, 38 percent had no opinion, while the remaining 32 percent correctly said he was opposed. In the same survey, 59 percent said that the issues involved in a nuclear freeze were too complicated for the public to decide (CBS, May 29–30, 1982).

### APPENDIX 1 – PUBLIC OPINION AND NUCLEAR WEAPONS

1. *The Gallup Opinion Index*, nos. 91–184 (January 1973–January 1981). *The Gallup Report*, nos. 185–225 (February 1981–June 1984).

2. *The Gallup Report*, no. 219 (December 1983): 3–5.

3. *The Gallup Report*, no. 220 (January–February 1984): 27–29.

4. The Gallup Poll, *Public Opinion 1979* (Wilmington, Del.: Scholarly Resources Inc., 1979), pp. 123, 195, 272.

### APPENDIX 2   THE IDEA OF SOCIAL WORTH

A persuasive argument could be made that, say, Brown's social worth is greater than Green's. But the relative social worth of Brown and Green presumably reflects how much of a contribution each has made to the well-being (or whatever) of others, for example, Jones and Smith. Suppose Brown contributed twenty units of well-being to Jones, the illiterate farm laborer, while Green generates ten units of well-being for Smith, the artist. Either we now continue an infinite regression by taking the relative social worth of Jones and Smith into account, or we adopt the axiom of equal intrinsic worth and conclude that Brown's contribution to net well-being (of Jones and Smith) is greater than Green's. We may not wish to attribute "social worth" to people on the basis of their relative contributions to the well-being of others, but — and this is the point — if we do then we must ultimately come to rest at an assumption about the intrinsic worth of different human beings. In short, we cannot escape the need for such an assumption by introducing the notion of social worth based on contribution.

# Notes

1. Meritocracy, a comparatively recent term, usually refers to a body of officials selected exclusively by merit and universal competition who, however, are at least nominally subordinate to others – a cabinet, president, legislature, and the like. In this sense, meritocracy might in principle be perfectly consistent with democratic control, provided only that democratically chosen rulers rule over the meritocracy. Thus meritocracy becomes equivalent to a bureaucracy based on merit. However, the alternative discussed in this chapter is a *regime* – meritocratic rulership – in which the rulers consist of a minority of those persons most qualified to rule, which by definition excludes the operation of the democratic process (except possibly as a *subordinate* process, in the way that the administrative process in a democracy is meant to be subordinate to the democratic process). Because of this possible ambiguity, I prefer to use Plato's more evocative term, though it may be less common in modern usage.

2. Some scholars, a minority, argue that Plato really intended to show the impossibility of a regime like that described in *The Republic*. It is surely true that on close textual analysis Plato's argument is more ambiguous and complex than it appears on the surface to be. Here I assume one possible interpretation and make no claim that it is the only reasonable interpretation.

3. Adolfo Sánchez Vásquez, *The Philosophy of Praxis* (London: Merlin Press, 1977).

4. On John Stuart Mill, see particularly Dennis F. Thompson, *John Stuart Mill and Representative Government* (Princeton: Princeton University Press, 1976). See also my "Procedural Democracy," in *Philosophy, Politics, and Society*, 5th series, edited by Peter Laslett and James S. Fishkin (New Haven: Yale University Press, 1979).

5. The theoretical issues involved in this distinction look to be quite intractable and I am aware of no satisfactory solution. For an effort to grapple with some of the issues, see my "Federalism and the Democratic Process," in *Liberal Democracy*, edited by John Chapman and Roland J. Pennock (New York: New York University Press, 1983).

6. Advocates of democracy and guardianship disagree, of course, about who, in general, can be expected to satisfy this requirement, a question central to the discussion in the next chapter. But they also disagree, and conceivably democrats might not entirely agree among themselves, on whether persons who may not *now* satisfy the requirement should nonetheless be admitted to full citizenship if it can be foreseen that participation may be necessary or sufficient for them to become qualified within some reasonable time. Depending on how they answer this question, they may also disagree on another: Suppose that members of some well defined group of people are not now qualified, but *no other persons* can be safely counted on to protect their interests. What is the best solution? In his *Considerations on Representative Government* (1865), J. S. Mill created this dilemma but never quite confronted it. He chose instead to contend that qualifications must take precedence over the benefits of participation. Many contemporary democrats would find his solution unacceptable.

7. These are essentially J. S. Mill's criteria. See the excellent discussion in Thompson, *Mill and Representative Government*, pp. 54 ff.

8. Garry Wills, *Inventing America: Jefferson's Declaration of Independence* (Garden City, N.Y.: Doubleday, 1978).

9. John Rawls, *A Theory of Justice* (Cambridge, Mass.: Harvard University Press, 1971), pp. 505 ff.

10. Since I have explored this theme elsewhere, I leave it undeveloped here. See my *Dilemmas of Pluralist Democracy* (New Haven: Yale University Press, 1982).

11. The question of obligation between generations, which has recently been taken up by philosophers, is, however, much more difficult than might appear. See, for example, John Rawls, *Justice*, and James S. Fishkin, "Justice Between Generations: The Dilemma of Future Interests," in *Social Justice*, edited by M. Bradic and D. Braybrook (Bowling Green, Ky.: Documentation Center, 1983).

## CHAPTER 3 – A CRITIQUE OF GUARDIANSHIP

1. Paul Bracken, *The Command and Control of Nuclear Forces* (New Haven: Yale University Press, 1983), pp. 197–201.

2. *Ibid.*, pp. 21–22, 69–71, 99.

3. *Ibid.*, p. 92.

4. *The Challenge of Peace: God's Promise and Our Response*, reprinted in *Origins* 13, no. 1 (May 19, 1983): 8. See also Bruce M. Russett, "Ethical Dilemmas of Nuclear Deterrence," in *International Security* 8 (Spring 1984): 36–54.

Russett was the "principal consultant" to the commission that produced the pastoral letter. The arguments of the letter, together with others, are analyzed in *The Security Gamble: Deterrence Dilemmas in the Nuclear Age*, edited by Douglas MacLean, Maryland Studies in Public Philosophy (Totowa, N.J.: Rowman and Allanheld, in press). The letter was severely criticized by Albert Wohlstetter, "Bishops, Statesmen, and Other Strategists on the Bombing of Innocents," *Commentary* (June 1981): 15–35.

5. Letter to Richard L. Simon, April 4, 1956. I am grateful to Fred R. Greenstein for providing me with a copy of this letter and to John S. D. Eisenhower for permission to quote from it.

6. *The Challenge of Peace*, p. 15.

7. Wohlstetter, *"Bishops, Statesmen, and Other Strategists,"* attributes this position to the bishops. Russett contends, in "Ethical Dilemmas of Nuclear Deterrence," that this is a misrepresentation, possibly based on reading earlier versions than the final one (p. 50, fn. 17).

8. George Sher arrives at this conclusion in "The U.S. Bishops' Position on Nuclear Deterrence: A Moral Assessment," in MacLean, *The Security Gamble.*

9. *The Challenge of Peace*, pp. 11–12.

10. *Ibid.* p. 15.

11. Bracken, *Command and Control of Nuclear Forces*, p. 161.

12. "[A]ny large-scale nuclear exchange, even of 'discriminating' weapons, would inevitably produce millions or tens of millions of civilian casualties. Numerous studies, drawing on private and governmental material, reach this conclusion. The combination of immediate casualties from blast and radiation with longer-term casualties . . . would be very great — even from attacks that were 'limited' to such 'strictly military' targets as the 1052 American and 1398 Soviet land-based ICBMs. Actually, the Defense Department's list of military and military related targets (40,000 of them, including 60 in Moscow alone) encompasses industry and utilities essential to the recuperation of the Soviet Union." Russett, *Ethical Dilemmas of Nuclear Deterrence*, p. 45. It should be noted that Russett introduced this information to show the difficulty of applying the principle of proportionality.

13. Even the principle that it is wrong to kill innocent people is more complex than it may seem, since it does not necessarily lead to the conclusion that killing innocent people is never morally permissible. In some situations all alternatives involve the certainty of death for some innocent people. And people vary in the relative degree of their innocence. See Gregory S. Kavka, "Nuclear Deterrence: Some Moral Perplexities," in MacLean, *The Security Gamble.*

14. Bracken, *Command and Control of Nuclear Forces*, p. 177.

15. *Ibid.*, p. 231.

16. "We perceive two dimensions of the contemporary dilemma of deterrence. One dimension is the danger of nuclear war with its human and moral costs. . . . The other dimension is the independence and freedom of nations and entire people. . . . The moral duty today is to prevent nuclear war from ever oc-

curring and to protect and preserve those key values of justice, freedom and independence which are necessary for personal dignity and national integrity." *The Challenge of Peace*, p. 17.

17. Bracken, *Command and Control of Nuclear Forces*, p. 239.

18. Studies have shown that in a great many fields the forecasts of experts are no better, or in some cases only slightly better, than the forecasts of laymen. One scholar, himself an expert on problems of long-range forecasting, concludes from the examination of a large number of systematic studies of the reliability of expert predictions in a great variety of fields: "Overall, the evidence suggests there is little benefit from expertise. And because improved accuracy shows up only in large samples, claims of accuracy by a single expert would seem to be of no practical value. Surprisingly, I could find *no* studies that showed an important advantage for expertise." J. Scott Armstrong, "The Seer-Sucker Theory: The Value of Experts in Forecasting," *Technology Review* (June/July 1980):21. Unfortunately, the inability of experts to make reliable forecasts does not seem to reduce their confidence in doing so, or the willingness of non-experts to treat their predictions with undeserved respect.

19. Bracken, *Command and Control of Nuclear Forces*, p. 113.

20. Bill Gulley, *Breaking Cover* (New York: Warner Books, 1980), p. 43, cited in Bracken, *Command and Control of Nuclear Forces*, p. 226.

21. John G. Kemeny, himself a mathematician, after chairing a presidential commission on the famous breakdown of the nuclear power station at Three Mile Island, observed: "In the course of our commission's work, we again and again ran into cases where emotions influenced the judgments of even very distinguished scientists. . . . I kept running into scientists whose beliefs border on the religious and even occasionally on the fanatical. . . . These people distort their own scientific judgments and hurt their reputations by stating things with assurance that they know, deep down, could only be assigned small probabilities. They become advocates instead of unbiased advisors. This is incompatible with the fundamental nature of science, and it creates an atmosphere in which there is a serious mistrust of experts: even when the hard evidence is overwhelming, if the issue is sufficiently emotional you can always get an expert to dispute it and thereby help throw all of science into national disrepute." "Saving American Democracy: The Lessons of Three Mile Island," *Technology Review* 83 (June/July 1980):70. For criticisms directly related to nuclear weapons, see Michael Walzer, "Deterrence and Democracy," *The New Republic* (July 2, 1984): 16–21.

22. The example and quotation above are from Daniel Kahneman and Amos Tversky, "Choice, Values, and Frames," *1983 APA Award Addresses* 39, no. 4: 3. See also their article, "Extensional Versus Intuitive Reasoning: The Conjunctional Fallacy in Probability Judgment," *Psychological Review* 90 (October 1983): 293–315.

23. *Considerations on Representative Government* (1861), edited by Currin V. Shields (New York: Bobbs-Merrill, 1958), p. 23.

## CHAPTER 4 – IS POLITICAL EQUALITY JUSTIFIED?

1. "Though I have said above . . . *That all Men by Nature are equal,* I cannot be supposed to understand all sort of *Equality: Age* or *Virtue* may give Men a just Precedency: *Excellency of Parts and Merit* may place others above the Common Level: *Birth* may subject some, and *Alliance* or *Benefits* others, to pay an Observance to those to whom Nature, Gratitude or other Respects may have made it due; and yet all this consists with *Equality,* which all Men are in, in respect of Jurisdiction or Dominion one over another, which was the *Equality* I there spoke of, as proper to the Business in hand, being that *equal Right* that every Man hath, *to his Natural Freedom,* without being subjected to the Will or Authority of any other Man." *Locke's Two Treatises of Government,* edited by Peter Laslett, 2nd ed. (Cambridge: At the University Press, 1970), *The Second Treatise,* p. 322.

2. In the *Second Treatise* Locke justifies the principle on the ground that there is "nothing more evident, than that Creatures of the same species and rank promiscuously born to the same advantages of Nature, and the use of the same faculties, should also be equal amongst one another without Subordination or Subjection, unless the Lord and Master of them all, should by any manifest Declaration of his Will set one above another, and confer on him by an evident and clear appointment undoubted Right to Dominion and Sovereignty" (p. 287). Locke denied any such "manifest Declaration" of God's will, conferred on anyone by "an evident and clear appointment" (for example, pp. 288–89). Thus Locke thrust the burden of proof on those who asserted a claim to inequality.

3. John Stuart Mill, *Utilitarianism and Other Writings* (New York: New American Library, 1962), p. 319.

4. John Rawls is a particularly interesting example because he explicitly rejects the premise and adopts in its place an assumption of the fundamental equality of all "moral persons." Yet he cannot finally dispense with the premise of equal worth in accounting for our obligations to persons who lack the qualities necessary for "moral personhood," such as children, for whom the deficiency is ordinarily not permanent, or feebleminded persons, for whom it is. *A Theory of Justice* (Cambridge, Mass.: Harvard University Press, 1971), pp. 29, 249, 505–506.

5. In some forms of Hinduism it is believed that people come into the world inherently unequal in worth because of differences in the relative purity or evil they have picked up through actions in their previous lives. A. H. Somjee, "Individuality and Equality in Hinduism," in *Equality,* edited by J. Roland Pennock and John W. Chapman (New York: Atherton Press, 1978).

6. *Intrinsic* worth must not be confused with *social* worth. See Appendix 2.

7. Douglas Rae, *Equalities* (Cambridge, Mass.: Harvard University Press, 1981), pp. 170 ff.

8. Though not identical, what follows is analogous to Mill's maxim, which he thought to be "of as universal truth and applicability as any general proposi-

tions which can be laid down respecting human affairs," that "human beings are only secure from evil at the hands of others in proportion as they have the power of being, and are, self-protecting." John Stuart Mill, *Considerations on Representative Government* (1861), edited by Currin V. Shields (New York: Bobbs-Merrill, 1958), p. 43. Since it was only by participating in their government, in Mill's view, that people could be fully self-protecting, he intended his principle to provide strong support for representative government.

9. The best treatment I know is James Fishkin, *Beyond Subjective Morality* (New Haven: Yale University Press, 1984).

10. Thomas Nagel describes "five fundamental types of value that give rise to basic conflict": specific obligations, such as those to friends or family; utility; general or universal rights; perfectionist values; and a commitment to one's own projects or life plans. No "single, reductive method or a clear set of priorities" exists for settling conflicts among them. *Mortal Questions* (Cambridge: At the University Press, 1979), pp. 129–34.

11. As James Grier Miller puts it, "A man with a head is something much more than a man's body plus his separate head." *Living Systems* (New York: McGraw-Hill, 1978), p. 44.

## CHAPTER 5 – VISION OF A POSSIBLE FUTURE

1. Quasi-guardianship in the sense used here should not be confused with proposals for advisory, consultative, or informational bodies like a "Science Court," or the organizations proposed below. In 1976, the Task Force of the Presidential Advisory Group on Anticipated Advances in Science and Technology, chaired by Arthur Kantrowitz, proposed the establishment of a Science Court that would provide a forum in which technical issues would be argued in an adversarial proceeding. Its function would be "to describe the current state of technical knowledge and to obtain statements founded on that knowledge, which will provide defensible, credible, technical bases for urgent policy decisions." The "judges" would be "established experts in areas adjacent to the dispute." They would issue a judgment on the dispute that would provide an "improved base on which political decisions could be reached through the democratic process." "Science Court Experiment: An Interim Report," *Science* (August 20, 1976): 653–56. See also A. Kantrowitz, "Controlling Technology Democratically," *American Scientist* (September–October 1975): 505–509. A Science Court would thus be a weaker and less complete solution to the problem of raising the level of civic competence than I propose below.

2. Benjamin Barber's *Strong Democracy* (Berkeley: University of California Press, 1984) appeared while I was revising these Abrams Lectures for publication. Barber strongly emphasizes the "functions of strong democratic talk." Sympathetic as I am with his wish to strengthen "democratic talk," his analysis and proposals do not seem to me to be adequate for the problem posed here.

The nine functions of strong democratic talk he describes all appear to presuppose that citizens possess whatever latent knowledge is necessary to make wise decisions in their own or the general interest, and that "talk" is sufficient to bring out what they already know. Since scientists and other specialists are also citizens, and would participate in the discussion, in one sense "talk" might be enough. To focus on discussion to the exclusion of learning by means other than, and in addition to, discussion seems to me to overestimate the contributions of "talk." However, some of his specific proposals are very similar to what I suggest below and the additional institutions I propose would undergird them with a higher level of civic learning.

3. After examining a number of textbooks on public policy analysis, Douglas C. Bennett concluded: "If you open a public policy textbook, particularly one elaborating the rational decision approach to policy analysis . . . you encounter almost complete silence about democracy. Despite the renewed attention to values in public policy analysis, some texts never even utter the word." Of a prototypical text, Bennett comments: "We can take it that [the authors] would not be more pleased if their text sat on office shelves in Sofia as well as Washington, nor if it were adopted for classes in Asunción as well as in Cambridge. Rather, this is a thoroughgoing statement of value neutrality, a central canon of the approach. . . . The utilitarian foundation of the rational decision approach . . . assumes that values are sharply distinct from facts and that rational discussion of values can only take place in the realm of values . . . that values are individual preferences, and these must be taken as 'givens' for each individual . . . that values are similar in character to one another, and in consequence the rational decision approach is neutral among them . . . that all values are continuous and fungible . . . [and] that social welfare is fully specified by aggregating individual preferences. Each of these assumptions is open to serious objection, and taken together they make it difficult for democracy to be considered in public policy analysis, or at least without significant distortion to what we mean by democracy." "Democracy and Public Policy Analysis," prepared for delivery at the Fifth Annual Research Conference of the Association for Public Policy Analysis and Management, October 20–22, 1983, Philadelphia, Pa.

4. Bureau of the Census, *Statistical Abstract of the United States 1982–83*, 103rd ed. (Washington, D.C., 1982), Table 934, p. 555.

5. Since our concern is with citizen competence, the term "citizen" is used in this discussion, though obviously much of what is described here would be available to any resident.

6. For example, Robert Paul Wolff, *In Defense of Anarchism* (New York: Harper & Row, 1970). Benjamin Barber also proposes a national initiative and referendum process, but integrated with other institutions intended to provide more information to voters than is usually available. *Strong Democracy*, pp. 281 ff.

7. Christopher Arterton has called my attention to the distinction between "plebiscitary" telecommunications — the term is his — and ways of using telecommunications that provide greater opportunities for dialogue. For providing me with information about some of the most important recent experiments

in the use of telecommunications to provide opportunities for participation, I owe much to discussions with him, to the research reports for the Project on Telecommunication Technologies and Political Participation which he headed, and to the report by Christopher Arterton, Edward H. Lazarus, John Griffen, and Monica C. Andres, *Telecommunication Technologies and Political Participation* (Washington: The Roosevelt Center for American Policy Studies, 1984), a draft of which the authors kindly permitted me to read. Their analysis is based on studies of experiences in twenty states, cities, or communities, each of which is described in a separate appendix.

8. John Griffen, "Report on Columbus Qube," *ibid.*

9. The simple technology has its drawbacks, since "calling in means that the viewer must stop watching to get through to the studio. Unless he/she gets through right away, the flow of conversation lags as questions formulated earlier on are asked later at an inappropriate time." John Griffen, "Report on Reading," *ibid.*

10. John Griffen, "Alaska's Legislative Teleconferencing Network," *ibid.*

11. If one defines as illiterate adults or those over eighteen years who have completed less than eight years of education, 16 percent of the total population of New York State residents eighteen years or over are functionally illiterate. In New York City the figure is about 21 percent. *New York Times* (March 27, 1984): 19.

12. *The New York Times*, December 11, 1983, sec. E, p. 8.

13. National Academy of Sciences, *Organization and Members 1981–1982* (Washington: National Academy of Sciences, 1981): x.

14. Commission on Behavioral and Social Sciences and Education, *CBASSE*, Washington, February 1984, p. 3.

15. These and other examples can be found in the monthly *News Report* published jointly by the two academies, the Institute of Medicine, and NRC.

16. *Early Transactions of the American Philosophical Society* (Philadelphia: The American Philosophical Society, 1969), p. 121.

17. Although their function is to help citizens, and not simply to make policy, to gain a better understanding of the alternatives, the advisory commissions would meet one of John G. Kemeny's recommendations based on his experience as chairman of a citizens' commission on Three Mile Island: "What's principally lacking on the federal scene, it seems to me, is the existence of respected, nonpartisan, interdisciplinary teams that could at least tell us what is possible and something about the pluses and minuses of different solutions. Take energy, for instance. What I would love to see established, with the National Academies or any other mechanism to confer respectability, is a team that will struggle the way our commission did and say, 'Okay, there are lots of suggestions around, and most of them won't work. But here are six different plans, any one of which is possible. We'll tell you what each one costs, what's good about it, what's bad about it, how dangerous it is, and what its uncertainties are.' At least each option would be a well-integrated, clearly thought-out plan. I would trust democracy — the president and Congress — to choose among them; but I do not

trust democracy to try to put together such a plan by having each committee of Congress choose one piece of it." "Saving American Democracy: The Lessons of Three Mile Island," *Technology Review* (June/July 1980):74.

18. The Science Court described above (Note 1) was to be adversarial. Although an adversarial process has some advantages, it presupposes that the relevant alternatives are reducible to two — for or against, guilty or not guilty. While the alternatives are sometimes dichotomous, they need not be. Adversary proceedings would force a dichotomy on choices that might better be seen as multiple — as Kemeny's comments in the preceding footnote suggest is the case with energy issues.

# Bibliography

American Philosophical Society. *Early Transactions of the American Philosophical Society*. Philadelphia: The American Philosophical Society, 1969.

Arterton, Christopher, Edward H. Lazarus, John Griffen, and Monica C. Andres. *Telecommunications Technologies and Political Participation*. Washington, D.C.: The Roosevelt Center for American Policy Studies, 1984.

Barber, Benjamin. *Strong Democracy*. Berkeley: University of California Press, 1984.

Bennett, Douglas C. "Democracy and Public Policy Analysis." Prepared for delivery at the Fifth Annual Research Conference of the Association for Public Policy Analysis and Management, October 20–22, 1983, Philadelphia, Pa.

Bracken, Paul. *The Command and Control of Nuclear Forces*. New Haven: Yale University Press, 1983.

"The Challenge of Peace: God's Promise and Our Response." *Origins* 13 (May 19, 1983): 1–32.

Commission on Behavioral and Social Sciences and Education. *CBASSE*. Washington, D.C. (February 1984).

Dahl, Robert A. "Federalism and the Democratic Process." In *Liberal Democracy*, edited by John Chapman and Roland J. Pennock. New York: New York University Press, 1983.

———. "Procedural Democracy." In *Philosophy, Politics, and Society*, 5th Series, edited by Peter Laslett and James S. Fishkin. New Haven: Yale University Press, 1979.

————. *Dilemmas of Pluralist Democracy*. New Haven: Yale University Press, 1982.

Fishkin, James S. "Justice Between Generations: The Dilemma of Future Interests." In *Social Justice*, edited by M. Bradic and D. Braybrook. Bowling Green, Ky.: Documentation Center, 1983.

————. *Beyond Subjective Morality*. New Haven: Yale University Press, 1984.

Griffen, John. "Report on Reading." In Arterton, *et al.*, *Telecommunication Technologies and Political Participation*. Washington, D.C.: The Roosevelt Center for American Policy Studies, 1984.

————. "Alaska's Legislative Teleconferencing Network." In Arterton *et al.*, *Telecommunication Technologies and Political Participation*. Washington, D.C.: The Roosevelt Center for American Policy Studies, 1984.

————. "Report on Columbus Qube." In Arterton, *et al.*, *Telecommunication Technologies and Political Participation*. Washington, D.C.: The Roosevelt Center for American Policy Studies, 1984.

Gulley, Bill. *Breaking Cover*. New York: Warner Books, 1980.

Kahneman, Daniel, and Amos Tversky. "Choices, Values, and Frames." *1983 APA Award Addresses* 39, no. 4: 10.

————. "Extensional Versus Intuitive Reasoning: The Conjunction Fallacy in Probability Judgment." *Psychological Review* 90 (October 1983): 292–315.

Kantrowitz, Arthur. "Controlling Technology Democratically." *American Scientist* (September October 1975): 653–56.

————. "Science Court Experiment: An Interim Report." *Science* (August 20, 1976): 505–509.

Kemeny, John G. "Saving American Democracy: The Lessons of Three Mile Island." *Technology Review* 83 (June/July 1980): 65–75.

Locke, John. *Locke's Two Treatises of Government*. 2nd ed. Edited by Peter Laslett. Cambridge: At the University Press, 1970.

MacLean, Douglas, ed. *The Security Gamble: Deterrence Dilemmas in the Nuclear Age*. Totowa, N.J.: Rowman and Allanheld. In press.

Mill, John Stuart. *Considerations on Representative Government*. Edited by Currin V. Shields. New York: Bobbs-Merrill, 1958.

————. *Utilitarianism and Other Writings*. New York: New American Library, 1962.

Miller, James Grier. *Living Systems*. New York: McGraw-Hill, 1978.

Nagel, Thomas. *Mortal Questions*. Cambridge: At the University Press, 1979.

National Academy of Sciences. *Organization and Members 1981–1982*. Washington, D.C.: National Academy of Sciences, National Academy of Engineering, Institute of Medicine, National Research Council, 1981.

Pennock, J. Roland, and John W. Chapman. *Equality*. New York: Atherton Press, 1978.

Plato. *The Dialogues of Plato*. Edited by B. Jowett. 2 vols. Vol. 1, *The Republic*. New York: Random House, 1937.

――――. *The Dialogues of Plato*. Edited by B. Jowett. 2 vols. Vol. 2, *Statesman*. New York: Random House, 1937.

Rae, Douglas. *Equalities*. Cambridge, Mass.: Harvard University Press, 1981.

Rawls, John. *A Theory of Justice*. Cambridge, Mass.: Harvard University Press, 1971.

Russett, Bruce M. "Ethical Dilemmas of Nuclear Deterrence." *International Security* 8 (Spring 1984): 36–54.

Sánchez Vásquez, Adolfo. *The Philosophy of Praxis*. London: Merlin Press, 1977.

Sher, George. "The U. S. Bishops' Position on Nuclear Deterrence: A Moral Assessment." In MacLean, *The Security Gamble*. Totowa, N.J.: Rowman and Allanheld. In press.

Somjee, A. H. "Individuality and Equality in Hinduism." In J. Roland Pennock and John W. Chapman, *Equality*. New York: Atherton Press, 1978.

Thompson, Dennis F. *John Stuart Mill and Representative Government*. Princeton: Princeton University Press, 1976.

Walzer, Michael. "Deterrence and Democracy." *The New Republic* (July 2, 1984): 16–21.

Wills, Garry. *Inventing America: Jefferson's Declaration of Independence*. Garden City, N.Y.: Doubleday, 1978.

Wohlstetter, Albert. "Bishops, Statesmen, and Other Strategists on the Bombing of Innocents." *Commentary* (June 1981): 15–35.

Wolff, Robert Paul. *In Defense of Anarchism*. New York: Harper & Row, 1970.

# Index

109

CONTROLLING NUCLEAR WEAPONS

was composed in 11-point Digital Compugraphic Caledonia and leaded 2 points by Metricomp;
with display type in Delphian by J. M. Bundscho, Inc.;
printed by sheet-fed offset on 55-pound, acid-free Glatfelter Antique Cream,
Smythe-sewn and bound over binder's boards in Joanna Arrestox B,
also adhesive bound with paper covers by Maple-Vail Book Manufacturing Group, Inc.;
and published by

SYRACUSE UNIVERSITY PRESS
SYRACUSE, NEW YORK 13210